Strange Tales of the Sea

Strange Tales of the Sea

Jack's Strange Tales Book 4

Jack Strange

Published 2016 by Creativia
Paperback design by Creativia (www.creativia.org)
Cover art by http://www.thecovercollection.com/

This book is dedicated to all lovers of the strange and mysterious

Contents

Introduction
Strange Tales of the Sea

Perhaps it is the sheer expanse of water, or the lack of knowledge of what lies beneath the surface, or the difference in lifestyles between seamen and landsmen, but the sea has often appeared a place of mystery. People standing on shore can see as far as the horizon, and until comparatively recently had no means of knowing what lay beyond. Once on board ship, men lived in a closed world, subject to the whim of the master and the lash of wind and waves. There was no pity at sea, and very little comfort; men lived on rough fare and in rough quarters.

Until the advent of steam and later motor engines, voyages could take weeks, months or sometimes years. Wooden ships powered by canvas sails probed into every corner of the world, from the bitter cold of the Arctic to the humid mouths of tropical rivers, from the endless expanses of the Pacific to the squall- ridden North Sea. In their off duty watches, or when they returned home and squandered their wages in shore side taverns, the seamen yarned. They spoke of the ships in which they had sailed and the captains that they had known, they spoke of events at sea and of the mysteries that added spice to their life. Much of what they said was exaggerated, or just plain fabricated, but there can be no doubt that every tale added to the lore of the sea. This little book relates some of these tales, and recalls a few of these mysteries.

Chapter Two
Haunted Ships

Ships, like houses, may be haunted, but while it is relatively easy to walk out of a haunted house, it is much more difficult to leave a haunted ship at sea. Perhaps for that reason, supposedly supernatural happenings on board a ship often appear more threatening than the land-based variety. Strangely, seaborne ghosts do not appear to have any time period; vessels of the twentieth century appear to have been as susceptible to haunting as those of the eighteenth or nineteenth, yet some of the more memorable stories appear from the Victorian era. Perhaps the Victorian cult of the dead and liking for Gothic romance may be blamed.

In April 1874 the ship *Harewood*, homeward bound from Pensacola in Florida arrived at the

Tail of the Bank, just downstream from Glasgow in Scotland. Some of the crew appeared in an agitated state, and soon the stories were circulating around the bars of the Broomielaw. The local press soon heard rumours that *Harewood* was haunted and a reporter began asking questions of the crew. One man, who had shipped aboard as an A. B. (Able-bodied seaman) gave his version of events. He said that after a few days he noticed that the hands were collecting in small groups, talking about the strange sounds that they had heard. He also mentioned hearing stories that the ship had once been named *Victoria* of London, and that there had been a murder on board.

Many seamen believed that it was bad luck to change the name of a ship, for such a procedure often brought bad luck. For instance when the owners of the German four masted barque *Rene Rickmers* changed her name to *Aland*, she was lost at New Caledonia on her very next voyage. It was not wise to tamper with such things, so there would be some superstitious fear about putting to sea in *Harewood*. That fear would be augmented with rumours of a murder. The seaman said that, although he worked as hard as ever, he found it hard to sleep, and he often heard the sounds of groaning, as if somebody was 'in deep distress.' One morning, he said, he awoke around dawn to see 'a figure standing' by his bunk. 'It was that of a young man, apparently about 27 years of age.' The seamen knew at once that the figure was not human; he also knew that it was a 'foreigner' but would not hurt him.

The figure stared at the seaman before it retreated 'into a corner and pointed to a livid mark round the neck.' All the time the figure's lips were moving 'as if in prayer.' After that the seaman frequently saw the figure, who spoke the same words again and again;

'I am not the man. I am not the man.'

It seemed that an elderly banker had been murdered on board *Victoria* of London and a man named Miller had been hanged for the crime. The seaman believed that this figure, which was seen 'gliding along the deck', on dark nights, but giving out 'a sort of phosphorescent light' was the ghost of the executed Miller, come to protest his innocence. 'I would not sail in that ship again for worlds' was the seaman's last word on the matter.

Sometimes the ghost on a vessel was known personally to the crew. It was common for a ghost to be a seaman who had once served on that vessel, but who had drowned, or been killed in some shipboard accident. This spectral mariner could lend his weight on a line when needed, or give advice during a storm. It was less common for the ghost to be unfriendly, although sometimes the crew would believe their extra hand to be the devil, complete with forked tail, cloven hooves and a smell of brimstone.

John Masefield the maritime poet mentioned a ghost on *John Elder*, a vessel built in Glasgow in 1870 for the Pacific Steam Navigation Company. According to Masefield, who probably heard from a crew member, the poop of *John Elder* was haunted, although the ship seemed to suffer no ill effects from the spirit. *Discovery*, who sits at Riverside in Dundee, is reputedly haunted. The light bulb above a bunk used by Ernest Shackleton blew without reason, and it is said he stalks the ship that he loved, but others think the ghost is of a seaman named Charles Bonner who fell from aloft in 1901.

In the early twentieth century British trawlers regularly travelled to fish in Icelandic waters. These were steam trawlers, with funnels so thin that they were known as 'woodbines' after the popular brand of cigarettes. Life on board these vessels was not comfortable, with the men berthed right forward, where the pitch and roll of the vessel could most easily be felt, and the skipper and mate right aft. In every kind of weather, the crew worked on an uncovered deck, gutting the fish, playing out the net, all in the teeth of wind that carried ice straight from the Arctic. The firemen had an equally harrowing time for they worked within a tiny space, shovelling coal into the boiler despite the frantic movement of the boat. They also had to clamber up on deck to dump the ashes, moving from extreme heat to sub-zero cold within the space of a minute. On one occasion a fireman was on deck when a massive wave broke over the vessel, sweeping him to his death. Yet something of him remained on board. His comrades often saw him working in the bunker, and whenever they came near to his berth, a ghostly voice sounded the warning, 'don't touch my bacca!' Although they had known him as a friend, other members of the crew refused to enter the bunker for the remainder of that voyage.

Large liners could also be haunted. At the beginning of the twentieth century, the most prestigious liners had four funnels but when *Titanic* was built, her fourth funnel was false, purely for effect. Before her maiden and final voyage some of the crowd saw an engineer inside this funnel, where no man ought to be. Some said that such an apparition was a bad omen. Another passenger steamer was blessed with an extra steward, who was seen gliding through the dining rooms. Legend speaks of the ghosts on the passenger liner *Utopia*. She was on her outward voyage from Italy and calling at Gibraltar when she collided with HMS *Anson*. As soon as *Utopia* began to go down, vessels and boats of all sizes arrived to help take off the passengers and crew, but many were still on board when she sank.

Utopia's owners could not afford to lose such a valuable ship, so had her salvaged, and she was towed into the dockyard at Gibraltar and refitted. As soon as it was practical, she returned to her previous work carrying passengers on cruises and trips. However, things were not all well. Passengers began to complain about strange sounds on board, and every time *Utopia* passed Gibraltar Bay passengers and crew experienced the sinking. They heard the sounds of rushing water and the cries and screams of people drowning. Not surprisingly, the stories spread, and fewer passengers used the ship. The owners even found it difficult to find crew, so eventually *Utopia* was sent to the breaker's yard. The ghosts had won the day.

Sometimes, however, the ghost met its match in a courageous officer of the watch. *Norfolk* was a Blackwall built ship, used for long haul passages from Britain. On one such voyage, she met dirty weather off Cape Horn and hove to until the weather moderated. While the Cape Horn snorter threw forty foot greybeards at them and every member of the crew working flat out to keep the ship afloat, nobody had time to worry about ghosts. However, as soon as the wind eased, some men heard an unusual noise. Not even the experienced Boatswain knew what it was, but one man likened it to the 'rattle in a dying man's throat.'

Superstitious as some seamen could be, the crew were far more unnerved with the unknown sound that they had been by the gale, and they began to see things that were not these. The atmosphere on *Norfolk* changed, so that when somebody began to scream during a night watch, men looked at each other in fear.

'What the hell's that?' The officer of the watch was a bold young man, brought up in the harsh practicalities of seamanship. He was not disposed to be afraid of man, the devil or any unidentified noise. Stalking forward, he ran up to the foc'sle-head and stopped as a ghastly apparition stood in front of him. The figure was pure white, with its arms raised high and a mass of black hair that seemed to flow from its head. All the time the figure was shouting:

'The vision of judgement! The vision of judgement!'

Near this terrible apparition, the lookout man cowered in terror in the lee of the weather cathead, covering his face behind cupped hands.

'Come out of that!' The officer of the watch demanded. Determined that nothing, ghost or human, would get the better of him on his own ship, he reached forward and grabbed the ghost, to find that his fingers gripped only flesh and bone. It was a woman, one of the third class passengers, and she had been driven mad by the strain of the voyage. Possibly the recent storm had unhinged already weak nerves. 'Come along now.' The officer escorted the woman to the ship's doctor, and immediately looked aloft as the mysterious rattle sounded again.

'I'll have no ghosts on my ship,' he growled, and ordered an immediate inspection of every inch of *Norfolk*. 'And you'll search until you find it,' he said, 'however long it takes!'

No doubt the seamen grumbled and swore, for that is the way at sea, but at last some anonymous man discovered the cause of the death rattle. One of the stays for the galley funnel had worked loose, and the wind was rattling the stay against the funnel. Once that was secured, *Norfolk* sailed on, once again a happy ship. The officer of the watch returned to his duty, a man who had only done his job in the best tradition of the British merchant navy.

Sometimes ghosts at sea could be benign or even welcome. Such was the experience of Mr Wilmot who was a passenger in the transatlantic steamer *City of Limerick*, crossing from Liverpool to New York in 1863. It was a stormy passage and for a while conditions were decidedly uncomfortable on board. When one gale at last began to ease Mr Wilmot clambered into his bunk and dreamed that his wife, who was safe on shore, visited him. She was wearing her nightdress and looked a little uncomfortable to see that her husband shared his cabin with another passenger, but she remained long enough to check that he was all right and then departed. When Wilmot awoke, his companion, Mr Tait, was shocked that a woman should visit him, for he too had seen Mrs Wilmot.

When Wilmot arrived in New York his wife said that she had felt very anxious for his safety about a week earlier and had crossed the sea to visit him in his cabin. She described the cabin exactly, and knew that Tait had been watching her all the time.

While British ships were home to ghosts, baleful or otherwise, Scandinavian vessels that sailed the North Sea and Baltic had their own guests. These vessels often had pixies or brownies on board, which could often be very welcome. One of the most fortunate ship in the early part of the twentieth century was named *Juno*, on board of who was a brownie. Many crewmen had seen the brownie holding the masts firm during the savage North Sea gales, and when the schooner *Fimma* ran into *Juno*, the brownie was seen running along the anchor cable to look after both vessels. The brownie helped *Juno* to be both a safe and a prosperous ship.

One of the most famous voyages of the nineteenth century was that of the American Joshua Slocum. As far as is known, he was the first man to sail solo around the world, in a time before modern yacht technology made such an event commonplace, before satellite navigation systems made the sextant redundant and before radios and air-sea rescue units made the seas comparatively safe. On the initial leg of his voyage from North America across the Atlantic, Slocum was taken ill and lay on the 'cabin floor in great pain.' While he lay there, he became aware of a strange man at the wheel of *Spray*. Afraid of pirates, Slocum approached the man, who doffed his cap and introduced himself as 'the pilot of the Pinta' and 'one of Columbus's crew.'

The pilot steered *Spray* to safety, and Slocum even had the presence of mind to record the song he sang:

'High are the waves, fierce, gleaming
High is the tempest roar!
High the sea-bird screaming!
High the Azore!'

Slocum was not alone to meet a ghost in the Atlantic, for this is one of the most ghost ridden oceans in the world, possibly because of the centuries of drama attached. As in the case of Slocum, the ghosts or apparitions or whatever they may be, can be helpful. According to legend, in 1828 a ship was bound to Newfoundland when the master glanced out of his cabin and saw a stranger lurking in one of the cabins. Suspecting that the man was a stowaway, the master lunged in, but although the man had disappeared, there was a message written on the wall:

Steer to the north west.

For a while the captain hesitated, but eventually he decided to alter course and shortly afterward saw a sinking ship. The only man on board was the stranger the captain had seen, and who said he had dreamed he was about to be saved.

Sometimes there were worse things than ghosts at sea. In 1913 the British ship *Johnson* was sailing off the Pacific coast of South America when she sighted a ship off Punta Arenas, Chile. As the ships closed the master of Johnson realised that the ship looked derelict and green moss covered her masts. According to the story, a party boarded the mysterious vessel and found her crewed only by twenty skeletons. The vessel was *Marlborough* of Glasgow, which had sailed from, Littleton in New Zealand in 1890 and had not been heard of since.

The tale of *Marlborough*, drifting unmanned across the Pacific for years, was mirrored in the legend of the American vessel *Star*, although some versions of the yarn have her named *Star of Dundee*.

Seamen are notoriously superstitious, so there was some discomfort on board when the schooner *Star* put to sea with a crew of thirteen men. However, it was the twentieth century, people were more sophisticated, and nobody really believed that sort of nonsense, did they? At first the voyage was fine, with the Pacific as smooth as the name suggested, the crew working with a will and *Star* performing as beautifully as schooners usually do.

However, as *Star* neared Midway Island, nearly in the centre of the Pacific, the weather turned foul. Great rollers rushed on the small vessel and the captain realised that they could not survive. When one particularly vindictive wave broke on board, he gave orders to abandon ship, just as *Star* ran aground on a coral reef. After a short while in the lifeboats, a passing barque rescued the crew and took them to Seattle, where they reported the loss of their vessel. *Star* was written off as just another casualty of the sea, and the crew signed on other vessels.

Six months later, the master of the ship *Doon* reported that *Star* was afloat, under full sail and heading to windward. The master of *Doon* was adamant that the vessel was *Star;* he knew her well. After a further three months an oil tanker sighted *Star,* seemingly in shipshape condition and only four hundred miles west of San Francisco. That meant that the schooner had sailed over two thousand miles from the reef where her crew had abandoned her. There were also rumours that she was manned. Some crewmen of the tanker swore that they had seen seamen on board *Star,* dressed in clothes that had gone out of fashion centuries previously.

By this time the legend of *Star* was well known in the Pacific, so ships were looking out for the mysterious schooner that refused to die. Now altering course, *Star* next appeared off Fanning Island, another three thousand miles across the Pacific, but again there was mention of men on board. This time the reports were more specific. *Star*'s new crew were dressed in the quilted doublets and baggy trousers of Elizabethan seamen.

By the time *Star* reached Hull Island, another thousand miles away, the story was better known. The schooner had piled onto a reef that had already claimed a victim. Back in the sixteenth century when Spain controlled half the sea lanes of the world, an English vessel had left the West Country to challenge King Phillip. She had a daring master and a bold crew, so rather than cruise the treasure ports of the Spanish Main, she had gone south, through Drake's Passage and into the virtually uncharted Pacific. Here the Spanish were most thinly spread, and pickings could be richer.

The English mariner cried havoc to the isolated ships of the Pacific. He ran up the west coast of the Americas, picking up prizes wherever he could, and then headed for the big one. Every year the Spanish sent two galleons from the Philippines to Mexico, large ships, well armed but crammed with treasure. There might be a hard fight, but the pickings would make any English privateer rich for life. Steering west, the Englishman headed for treasure and glory, but he did not know the true nature of the Pacific.

A storm blew up, driving the already battered ship before it, until she piled up on an unknown reef near Midway. There the master and crew waited for another vessel. For centuries they waited, until the American schooner *Star* came ashore, and the Elizabethan mariners, long since dead and decayed, took over. Now they were roaming the Pacific, still without a chart, still hunting for prey.

Star continued to cruise, possibly carried by the tides and currents of the Pacific, possibly crewed by the Elizabethan phantoms, until, four years after they had been abandoned by her American crew, she again ran aground on the same reef off Midway Island. This time, however, there was no reprieve and the great Pacific waves battered her to pieces.

There were other drifting ships at sea. *Wyer D. Sargent* was a 1520 ton schooner built in Sedgewick, Maine in 1888. In March 1891 Captain Danse commanded her on a voyage from Lagana with a cargo of Mexican mahogany worth around £7000. She was caught by a terrible storm off North Carolina on 31 March and lost all three masts so she rolled back and forth, unhampered and free. Fortunately a Norwegian vessel saw her plight and rescued her crew, leaving *Wyer D. Sargent* to sink, but the derelict had her own ideas.

Possibly kept afloat by the pressure of her cargo on her hull, the schooner floated here and there across the Atlantic, being sighted a recorded 27 times in the following two years. She was seen off Bermuda in the summer of 1891 and vessels were launched to try and salvage her for the sake of her cargo, but she slipped away into the waste of ocean.

She crossed the Gulf Stream at least twice and was sighted on both sides of the ocean in her pilotless surge from the New to the Old World and back. On 12 October 1892 the steamer *Asiatic Prince* saw her 900 miles east of Bermuda. At that time she was virtually waterlogged, with her decks awash with water but so far down by the stern that her bows were clear of the sea, with her anchor swinging loose.

Wyer D. Sargent continued to drift, derelict and dangerous, for a further four years before finally

grinding ashore at Conception, an uninhabited island in the Bahamas in early 1897.

There were other well travelled derelicts including the American schooners *Twenty-one Friends*
and *W. L. White*. The crew abandoned *W. L. White*
during a blizzard off Delaware Breakwater in 1888.
She drifted the full width of the Atlantic to come
to grief in the Outer Hebrides. *Twenty-one Friends*
was seen 21 times in a year and then vanished,
presumed sunk.

However, there is no telling when ghosts or
ghostly vessels could reappear; they are just one
strange tale of the sea.

Chapter Three
Stowaways

There is something romantic about stowing away on a ship, hiding on a vessel that will take one to an unknown destination, either for adventure, or in the hope of starting a new life, or to escape from a country or place that has become intolerable.

Certain types of ships seemed to attract stowaways. The whaling ships from Dundee did, for instance, although why anybody would want to stow away on a ship that operated in some of the worst seas in the world, in some of the worst conditions, doing a job that was always dangerous and often bloody, is anybody's guess. The whaling ship's masters were not unduly harsh with the youngsters they found, but nor did they treat them with kid gloves. The usual response was to land them at the nearest port, wherever that was, so it was quite possible that a lad of ten or eleven was put ashore in Orkney or Shetland with a ship's biscuit and no way to get back to Dundee. There was at least one occasion when a stowaway was simply put in a passing fishing boat and left to the tender mercies of the fishermen, and Scottish fishermen were not renowned for their gentleness.

If that sounds a bit harsh, think of what happened to another man who tried to stow away. In the 1880s, *Professor Woermann* sailed regularly from Hamburg to Great Britain, with an occasional trip to West Africa. In November 1883 she had made one of her longer voyages and was at Little Popo in West Africa; the crew were unloading their cargo bale by bale when somebody shouted for the captain.

There was a body on board. At first there was a horrible suspicion of murder, but then the captain put all the facts together. They had found a man lying dead on the deck of the hold, with the bales piled around him to make a natural cave or hollow. He had an empty bottle of gin beside him, and the bone of a leg of lamb, but he was stone dead. It seemed that he had died of thirst.

The captain worked out what had happened: the man had waited until the ship had been loaded in Hamburg and had sneaked on board. He had secreted himself in the hold with enough food, he thought, for the short voyage from Hamburg to Britain, hoping to start a new life there. However the voyage was much longer and his food and drink ran out, so he must have lain there in the dark, not knowing what was happening and without any means of calling for help, slowly dying. There were no identification papers on him, so that man's identity was never discovered.

Chapter Four
Strange Bells

Isn't it strange how important bells are? The sound of church bells can be evocative as they peal out over the surrounding countryside; some were endowed with near magical qualities and even named. Big Ben springs to mind; the name is of the bell, not the tower in which it sits.

Nautical bells were also vital. They marked the passage of the hours during the agonising passages of the doldrums and during tropical storms and Arctic frost. They were also handy as fog horns in vessels that did not have such an instrument, and when the whaleboats were out hunting in the broken ice and floes of the Arctic, the bell could mark the position of the whaling ship.

Ship's bells were usually made of brass; their peals were known as 'bells' as the 24 hour day on board a ship was divided into six watches, with each half hour marked by the peal of the bell. Eight peals – eight bells – marked the end of each watch except for the first dog watches, which was marked by four bells.

Ship's bells have a habit of surviving. When *Great Britain* was beached on the Falkland Islands her bell was removed and used outside the cookhouse at Goose Green. Gugh in the Scilly Islands had a ship's bell in the church; legend claims that local wreckers lured a French ship onto the island and looted her when she beached, but the money they raised was used to build the church. Eriskay in Orkney has a church bell that was salvaged from a German warship in Scapa Floe.

Sometimes they had a long history; the bell of one of the first screw steamers to cross the Atlantic was salvaged and used on a store ship during the Crimean War before being hung at the Bethel ship at Alexandria, where it was used to summon the Christian seamen to worship in that essentially Islamic city. From there it travelled to Ruthrieston Parish Church in Aberdeen in 1893: it may yet still be there.

There are many legends of other bells that travelled by sea. There was Great Tom, the Kentsham Bell that was said to be the largest bell that was ever sent to England. There are a number of bells known as Great Tom in England: Great Tom of Tom Tower, Christchurch in Oxford and Great Tom of Lincoln being two of them but the Kentsham Tom was the bell that caused all the problems. The ship carried Great Tom of Kentsham without any problems, but when the unloading began, things started to go wrong.

Great Tom was raised from the ship and was being transferred to land, the ship master swore. At that very instant the rope snapped and the bell splashed into the water and sunk. There was great consternation among the local people and they asked a local wise man what they should do. He gave the sound advice that they should take 'six yoke of white miche-kine which have never borne the yoke, and take fresh withy bands which have never been used before, and let no man speak a word either good or bad until the bell is at the top of the hill.'

They did exactly as they were ordered and hauled the bell out of the sea and onto dry land. Then they whipped up the oxen until they hauled the huge bell inch by inch to the top of the hill where the church stood empty and waiting. The ship master had been watching closely, biting his lip with nervousness as the bell had creaked and groaned its way up the hill. As soon as it was safe, he opened his mouth and shouted:

'In spite of all the devils in hell

We have got to land old Kentsham's Bell'

The holy man looked at him in horror but it was too late: the damage had been done. The withy bands snapped and the bell rolled away down the hill, scattering all the people who had watching and laboured and waited with such hope. They watched as it bounced into the sea and vanished forever, but sometimes, on a dark night or when the tide is right, the sound of its tolling can be heard from deep beneath the waves. There is a similar tale from Boscastle in Cornwall, when a bell was shipped for the church but when the pilot thanked God for the safe passage the ship master laughed at his Christianity and said it was his own skill that got them there.

'May God forgive you' said the pilot.

Just as he had spoken a huge wave rose from the depths of the sea and overwhelmed the ship. The vessel sank but the tolling of the bell continued and when a storm is expected, the bells are still heard as a warning to those who mock God. There is another tolling bell at Bosham where the Norse stole the bell from a monastery; their ship sank in the Bosham Channel in the Bell Hole and the bell is still heard.

Wales too has its tolling bell. In Cardigan Bay was a line of rocks at the Lleyn Peninsula. They were known as St Patrick's Causeway and sup-posedly led to the Lowland Hundreds, long since flooded by the sea, but whose church bells can still be heard by those with the power to hear.

There are hundreds of other superstitions of course, such as the belief that bringing bananas on board a fishing boat will destroy any hope of a decent catch. Flowers were equally unwelcome, as were some church ministers, as both had connec-tions with funerals. Sharks following ships were often taken as a portent of a death about to occur on board. Carrying an empty coffin was also a sure way of ensuring that there would be a death on board before the end of the voyage. However, with or without a coffin, there were often deaths on ships at sea. In these cases the Sailmaker sewed the corpse into a sail, with the last stitch always through the nose. The body was then slid overboard after an appropriate ceremony; on a warship there would be a couple of cannon balls at the feet so it would sink. There was little more damaging for morale than to have the body of a shipmate floating in the ship's wake, gradually being eaten by fish or sharks.

Nautical traditions may have been strange, but there was usually a firm basis of sense behind them.

Chapter Five
Ships With Ghosts and Ships With Luck

There are no specific seas where ghost ships predominate; they can be found in most areas of the world. For instance there was a spectral ship seen off Abergele in Wales that was rumoured to be *Gwennon Gorn* of Prince Madoc and there are phantom ships in the Great Lakes between Canada and the United States of America, with *Griffon* and *Edmund Fitzgerald* haunting these difficult waters.

It is possible that ghost ships are only optical illusions, mirages created by the same refraction of light rays that causes oases to appear to travellers in the desert, but sometimes the tales are well documented. Although the tales have certainly improved in the telling, the essential core has an element of truth. Take for instance the story of the *Flying Dutchman.*

Possibly the most famous sighting of this phantom ship was by HMS *Bacchante* in the late 19th century. The log entries read like this:

At 4 AM she crossed our bows. A strange, red light, as of a phantom ship all aglow, in the midst of which light the broken masts, spars and torn sails of a brig, 200 yards distant, stood out in strong relief as she came up with us.

The look-out man on our foc'sle reported her as close to the port bow, where also the officer of the watch from the bridge clearly saw her, as did the quarter-deck midshipman, who was sent forward at once to the foc'sle, but on arriving there no vestige, nor any sign whatever of any material ship could be seen.

This reported sighting is unique as it was made by intelligent, sober officers on a vessel of the Royal Navy, in which the future King George V also served. However, other men of equally good character and unimpeachable integrity have also reported seeing such a phantom at various times in the past.

Most people in the Western world have heard of the *Flying Dutchman*, that legendary vessel doomed forever to round the Cape of Good Hope, but few will realise that the seas are haunted by a number of other, equally mysterious vessels. For instance there is *Lady Lovibond*, an 18th century vessel that was wrecked on the Goodwin Sands off Kent on the 13th of February 1748. Legend tells of a honeymoon on board the ship, with a jealous rival who murdered the groom before running the ship onto the Sands. Every fifty years thereafter, on the anniversary of the shipwreck, *Lady Lovibond* was said to reappear, heading for the Sands with her wedding party on board. Even without *Lady Lovibond*, the Goodwin Sands are a dangerous place. Nobody knows how many ships have ended their careers there, but legends speak of thousands of mariners having perished on these treacherous sandbanks, so it is not surprising that they should be haunted. There are ghosts off Ireland too, where spectral ships of the Spanish Armada occasionally appear.

Other phantom vessels have been seen in British waters. There is said to be a ghostly full rigged ship that sails the North Channel off the Mull of Galloway. *St Garva* sighted this vessel as it sailed across her bows and vanished. Unlike the *Flying Dutchman*, there does not seem to be any aftermath of misfortune, so perhaps she was merely a ship running home.

While the *Flying Dutchman* has a whole host of legends attached to her, of the master gambling with the devil, of a crew of skeletons, of blasphemy committed, most other vessels have no such history. When British trawlers worked in far northern waters there were many stories of ghostly fishing boats seen trawling in horrendous conditions. At one time fishing boats were able to work just off the coast of Britain and return within a few hours, but overfishing forced them further and further away to seek new grounds. By the early years of the twentieth century British boats fished anywhere from the Grand Banks of Newfoundland to the White Sea. Weather and sea here could be so extreme that it was no surprise that many boats were lost.

Fishermen knew the Continental Shelf off North West Norway as the Wall of Death, for the sea bed dropped suddenly from a couple of hundred fathoms to a seemingly bottomless pit. Even worse was the passage near the Lofoten Islands. If the boat were vastly unfortunate, she would meet a westerly Atlantic gale at the same time as an Easterly was blowing from West Fiorden. In that case, even the Norwegian Pilot recommended that 'no vessel should enter' the passage between Lofotodden and Hogholman. There is one recorded message from a British trawler that was the victim of an Icelandic 'blinder,' which ran 'Boat gone. Funnel gone. Hope gone. Good Bye England.'

It was hardly surprising, given these conditions, that overstrained trawler men should see ghost ships. There were many stories of ghostly trawlers sailing in horrendous conditions, with moonlight reflecting off Otter Boards and shadowy crews in phosphorescent oilskins. Yet few of these vessels had names; nobody could identify them as lost boats.

Nevertheless, one ghost ship that was easily identifiable was the Scarborough smack *Northern Star*. In February 1891 *Northern Star* was in collision with the liner *Bravo* a few miles off Hull. Believing her to be badly damaged, the crew took to the lifeboats, leaving *Northern Star* to float, derelict, on the North Sea. The currents took hold of her, and after a few days she was driven ashore on the rocks at the village of Catterline, about fifteen miles south of Aberdeen. After a quick inspection, it became apparent that *Northern Star* was in reasonable condition and could be salvaged, provided that she was taken off the rocks

At that time, every village along the coast had some connection with the fishing industry, so the authorities asked the local fishermen to board *Northern Star* and bring her into harbour. They refused.

'Why not?' The authorities asked, as mighty waves began to pound the timbers of the smack.

'That's a phantom ship,' they said, 'we'll no' be going aboard her.'

Desperate to salvage something, the authorities resorted to the argument they knew best. 'We'll pay you,' they said, 'four shillings an hour if you go on board and rescue the ship's stores.'

Four shillings an hour was a phenomenal amount of money, equal to four days' pay for a soldier or a very good day at the herring fishery for a fisherman. But still the fishermen refused. They had it in mind that *Northern Star* was a ghost ship, and nothing would change their mind. Lacking the skill, or the courage, to board the smack themselves, the forces of Authority could only watch as the North Sea gradually destroyed *Northern Star*, complete with her precious cargo.

Another North Sea legend is the phantom of the German submarine U-116. She sunk on the 28th October 1918, nearly at the end of the First World War, and nobody was sure why. She was sighted on many occasions later, always when the weather was bad. She ran on the surface, with a crew of skeletons on her conning tower and carried a message of future ill tidings.

A second Great War U-boat was known as an unlucky ship even before she began her career of murder under the high seas. U-65 was built at Bruges in Belgium and while she was being built a girder killed one of the dockyard workers. Such an inauspicious start was unfortunate, but her ill luck was compounded on her sea trials, when poisonous fumes suffocated three men in the engine room. The German high command did not release such news, and U-65 entered the Imperial German Navy, but her evil fortune continued. When her captain ordered a man forward to inspect the hatches, he unaccountably stepped overboard and drowned before he could be rescued. The captain ordered a dive, but rather than levelling at five fathoms U-65 slipped down to the sea bed and remained there for twelve hours as the crew began to panic and water and battery fumes seeped in. As enigmatically as she had sunk, she rose again to the surface. An inspection found nothing wrong to U-65 returned to duty, but during routine rearming a torpedo exploded, killing the second lieutenant and five crewmen. Although he was dead, the second lieutenant returned to oversee U-65 being towed into dry dock for repairs, standing with his arms folded on the deck.

The presence of the officer so alarmed another crewman that he deserted before the submarine returned to her patrol around the Straits of Dover. The ghostly officer remained, terrorising the officers and crew even more than the Royal Navy did. Eventually U-65 sailed back to her base, but a

British aerial attack killed the captain. At last the Imperial German Navy acknowledged that there was a problem and sent a priest to exorcise the boat. However the troubles continued. When U-65 returned to the war one man committed suicide, another lost his sanity and the chief engineer broke his leg.

On the 10th July 1918 the American submarine 1-2 reported seeing U-65 drifting off Cape Clear with a single officer standing on the deck, standing with his arms folded. As the American vessel prepared to attack the U boat blew up. There were no survivors.

Naturally, other coasts and other seas have their quota of ghost ships. A Dutch vessel named *Palantine* was driven onto the coast of Rhode Island in 1752. Almost immediately, local fishermen pushed off from shore to rescue the emigrants, struggling through the surf with their terrified human cargoes. Once the passengers were safe, the fishermen returned to strip the ship of anything valuable. Laughing, they set fire to the wreck, partly for the fun of the thing, partly to cover up their crime. Only when they set off, boats loaded with booty, on their final voyage home, did they see the woman on deck. Fear had driven her below, where she had hidden from the looters. Now she stood on deck as the flames burst around her. *Palantine* burned to the waterline, but she has often been seen since, burning off the coast of Rhode Island.

It is possible that unlucky ships were even more frightening. Every seaman knew that ships could be lucky or unlucky. Even before the boat was built, there were decisions to make. In some ports of the Moray Firth, people believed that chestnut, or 'she oak' was a powerful wood that's ailed faster at night than during the day, while many boats incorporated ash or rowan wood to protect the boat from witchcraft. The shipwright could tell by the feel of his adze on the timber of the keel, if the boat was lucky or unlucky and once cursed, or blessed, a ship was forever stuck with her reputation. Nevertheless, there were certain ways of obtaining good luck for a boat. Scottish fishermen habitually rowed or sailed their boat sun-wise, or 'west-about' as soon as they left the harbour and this practise still continues in some east coast fishing stations.

There were also lucky and unlucky days. In some fishing villages, such as Crovie, marriages were always held on a Saturday, followed by a week when the groom did not go to sea. Fishermen expected the weather to change on a Friday, but it was usually considered unlucky to fish on a Sunday, except at Prestonpans in East Lothian where that day was considered the best for fishing. Obviously, lucky days also extended to boatbuilding. In Scotland, Friday was the best day for laying the keel, and often Thursday was a lucky day for launching, while in Boulogne, it was unlucky to make any major alterations once the work had started. In many places, a minister would bless a boat for luck, but Scottish fishermen believed that a minister was unlucky. In many places around the Mediterranean, ships could not be launched on a Friday. There is one school of thought that believed that this superstition spread from the Muslims, who believe that Adam was created and expelled from the Garden of Eden on a Friday, which is also to be the day of Resurrection.

Both merchant ships and warships could carry luck. The Royal Navy, one of the most professional and successful of all navies, did not deign to use a name thought lucky or discard one that brought misfortune. Perhaps the most commonly told example, and virtually certainly apocryphal, is the story of the ship *Friday*. According to the story, the navy was determined to end the superstition that said Friday was unlucky. They commissioned a ship named Friday, laid the keel on a Friday, gave the command to a Captain Friday and she sailed on her maiden voyage on a Friday. The story claims that she disappeared on that same voyage.

Other vessels were undoubtedly unlucky. In June 1893 HMS *Camperdown*, a 10,600 ton battleship was engaged in naval manoeuvres in the eastern Mediterranean off Tripoli. Possibly owing to a mistake by Vice Admiral Sir George Tryton, she sunk her ram deep into HMS *Victoria*, one of two Victoria class battleships. Thirteen minutes after the collision HMS *Victoria* crumpled and sank with the loss of 358 of her crew. Only 357 were rescued. Sir George Tryton remained on the bridge and went down with his ship, with legend declaring that he said 'it was all my fault.'

It was now that the legend of unlucky ships merged with that of sea ghosts, for at exactly the same time as *Victoria* sank, a few minutes after three-thirty in the afternoon; Lady Tryton was giving a party in her house at Eton Square in London. Many of the guests saw the Admiral walk down the stairs, although his wife told them he was at sea.

One of the unluckiest vessels was *Great Eastern*, a vessel of over 18,000 tons at a time when a large ship might weight 5000 tons. There were so many problems on her construction that John Scott Russell, one of her builders, was financially ruined, while Isambard Brunel, her designer, experienced a heart attack on her deck and passed away before her launch in 1858.Six men died during her building while there were rumours of a riveter and his apprentice disappearing; even when she was launched she was so reluctant to move from her berth that special cranes were brought in.

The maiden voyage of *Great Eastern* was equally unsuccessful, as an explosion on board killed five men; two more men drowned and a third was found dead in his bunk. By this time men were beginning to name her the 'blood thirsty giantess.' On her return voyage across the Atlantic *Great Eastern* ran into a nasty storm, and while in Cork Harbour an unexplained kick of her helm killed the quartermaster. Later she ran aground off Long Island. Her luck did not change, so her career was short. When she was scrapped in 1889, the skeletons of the riveter and his apprentice were discovered within her double hull. The scrap metal was sold for one thirteenth of her original cost. It might be interesting to find out on what the metal was used.

The schooner *Finstrom* was also unlucky. At her launch at Aaland in 1920, she sped across the narrow inlet where she was built and ran aground on the opposite shore. She ran aground on Gotland on her maiden voyage to England, and never sailed again. *Fimma* was another unlucky Aaland schooner. Even before she was rigged in 1874, she drifted loose and rammed another vessel, while her mate, Mattias Mattson, saw a coffin in her wake. He immediately sought another ship, which was fortunate for *Fimma* sank on her first summer voyage into the White Sea.

Sometimes seamen turned to women to help cure an unlucky vessel. If Yorkshire fishermen believed that their boat was unlucky, their wives would gather at midnight, kill a pigeon, cut out the heart and prick it with needles. The women then roasted the heart over the glowing embers of a fire in the hope of luring the evil spirit from the cursed boat. When the women believed that the spirit had arrived, they offered it presents to remain away from the boat.

To balance the unlucky vessels, some ships had a reputation for good luck. One such was the barque *Lawhill*, named after the hill that overlooks Dundee. In the 1920s the Gustaf Eriksson Line owned her and one example of her luck came when she was in Buenos Aires. Of the sixty vessels in harbour, only *Lawhill* succeeded in obtaining a cargo. Another lucky vessel was the aircraft carrier *Ark Royal*. The Germans named her as a prime target during the Second World War, and periodically reported her as sunk, much to the amusement of her crew. On frequent occasions Lord Haw Haw asked where *Ark Royal* was, to which her crew, crowded around the radio, responded 'here we are! Here we are!' Eventually the aircraft carrier was torpedoed, but even then *Ark Royal* looked after her crew. She took twelve hours to sink, ensuring that her crew had time to escape.

Chapter Six
Crimps, Prostitutes and Lodging Houses

There was no secret that the British seaman was often hard used when at sea, but until the 19th century, not much attention was paid to him ashore. Basically he was left to his own devices, often to fall prey to the avaricious predators that lurked around the docksides. However expert he was up aloft in the screaming hell of a Cape Horn snorter; however staunch he was when faced with interlocking floes of ice in the Davis Straits, or when an Atlantic storm blew his vessel onto the merciless Hebridean rocks, he was often a babe on shore.

The dockside pubs and lodging houses were full of sharks that were ready to prey on naïve Jack ashore. There were other places throughout the world that were renowned for their treatment of seamen: Strait Street or Strada Stretta in Valetta was one, full of bars, bordellos and dancing halls. Known as the 'Gut', Strait Street saw gentlemen duelling with swords in the early 19th century and servicemen brawling with fists on any evening. The prostitutes of Strait Street had a reputation for fun and frolics; one of their tricks, as late as the 1950s and perhaps later, was to snatch the cap from a sailor's head, throw it into their brothel and seduce the man who followed his cap. The Cairo was famous among British seamen in the 20th century, complete with its drag queens and Maltese entertainers; visiting American sailors frequented the Britannia, an underground restaurant.

Ratcliffe Road in London was another street popular with shore bound sailors. The prostitutes of Ratcliffe Road could be extremely friendly, or the exact opposite. It was not unknown for some friendly and honest women to team up with a seaman after a long voyage and act as his wife as long as his wages lasted. It was an arrangement that benefitted them both; she would be scrupulously honest with his money and would act as his wife and housekeeper, while he supplied the money. As soon as the money ran out, the seaman would wake up one morning on board a ship, and his temporary wife would be seeking her next husband.

There was a street in Dundee named Couttie's Wynd, where the ladies of the night would entice seamen into a darkened room and either pick their pockets while they lay drunk on the bed, or have a couple of hefty male friends pummel him into unconsciousness while the lady searched him for anything valuable.

Such treatment was bad enough, but paled into insignificance when compared to the vicious practise of crimping that was commonplace in some ports, and was widespread on the west coast of the United States. Some crimps had colourful names such as Shanghai Brown, but that name should have been warning enough. The term 'to Shanghai' meant to dupe, drug or disable a seaman and ship him onto some hell ship bound for the far corners of the world. In the 19th and early 20th century, crimps virtually controlled the recruitment of seamen in many ports, particularly along the west coast of America. Often the ship master worked hand in hand with the crimp and both benefit. The crimp was also known as a boarding house master, or mistress, and they waited for ships to come into port and seamen to fall into their predatory claws. The system was simple but evil; the ship master could haze the men until the deserted without their pay, or simply delayed payment until the crew were so frustrated they deserted for another ship,

In 1889, 411 British seamen deserted their ships in New York alone, unpaid and alone in an alien port, but the west coast was far worse, with San Francisco notorious as the worst port on the coast. It may seem strange that seamen would be willing to desert at the end of a voyage, knowing that they would forfeit the wages of a voyage that might have lasted for up to eight or nine months. However, the men had been confined inside a ship for that length of time, with much of their off duty hours in the cramped claustrophobia of the forecastle. In this tiny space, with less allowance of air than a convicted murderer, the seamen slept, yarned, played cards and dreamed of a run ashore. Seamen in general and British seamen in particular had one well-known vice: drink. The less scrupulous shipmasters and all the boarding masters knew and exploited this well.

When the ship arrived in port, the captain would allow the boarding masters on board. The boarding masters would supply the crew with a great deal of drink and the promise of willing women. After a while, still not paid, the part stupefied men would follow the crimps to worship at the joint temple of Bacchus and Aphrodite. As they left before the official termination of their articles – their contract – they were not entitled to their wages, which reverted to the owners of the ship. The ship master possibly got his percentage of the money.

The seamen would go to the lodging house of the boarding master. He would be fed drink and the company of women. After a few days the crimp would kindly find him another ship, for a fee. In the more extreme cases the seaman would be drugged and wake up on a blood boat, a hell ship with a nightmare for a captain and a bully mate who enforced discipline with belaying pin and brass knuckles.

The seaman therefore found himself on board a ship outward bound and in debt to the boarding master. He was therefore working for nothing for some time, with a consequent loss of morale and efficiency. In many cases ship masters worked hand in glove with boarding masters; the captain paid the crimp a tidy sum for every seaman he could supply, and in return got a crew of half doped, reluctant and disgruntled men who could be battered into shape by a bully mate.

This strange tradition of the sea no longer exists in Western ports in the 21st century. Union regulations and more strict government laws have clamped down on crimping. Life is better for the loss.

Chapter Seven
A Brace of Ships: Madagascar and Betsy Cairns

In 1850 the population of Victoria in Australia was 76,000. A mere decade later 538,000 people lived in the colony and others were eager to travel there. It was not an easy journey, for twelve thousand miles of often dangerous sea separated Britain, from where the vast bulk of emigrants originated, and Australia. Augmenting the distance was the discomfort, for most emigrants travelled steerage class, packed into shocking accommodation with bad food, the chance of disease and constant sea-sickness. There was one case of a woman who spent the entire voyage being sick, only to die as soon as she reached Australia.

Once the emigrants arrived, things were not much better. The largest Victorian city of Melbourne was not much better than a large town, and outside was little but heat, bush and insects. Even the people were considered as primitive, for Australia still had the reputation of a convict colony where bushrangers roamed what roads there were. Nonetheless, there were compensations. Land was cheap, work was available and, more important, there was gold.

As soon as gold strikes were made in 1850, yellow fever gripped Australia as vast numbers of people rushed towards the diggings. Despite local employers raising pay, men removed their quills from the inkwell for one last time, or abandoned their sheep on the fields and bought pick, shovel and provisions for the gold fields. Gigs, drays and carriages rattled along the Australian roads, filled with diggers who had once been barristers or clerks, lawyers or policemen, while the ordinary labourer struggled on foot, choking in their dust.

When clipper ships carried the news of gold to Britain, there was an immediate exodus. The emigrant trade boomed as people, mainly single men, got passage to Australia by any means that they could. While many sailed as bona-fide passengers, others posed as seamen, hoping to desert for the gold fields as soon as they arrived.

It was a busy time for shipping. As well as ferrying thousands of passengers across three oceans, ships were also carrying back the products of the gold fields. The gold was often escorted on board, to be secreted in specially made compartments under the master's cabin. Some of these cargoes were phenomenally valuable, with ships carrying up to one million pounds worth of gold. Fast ships were preferred for this task, for the owners of the gold wanted to have it banked safely in Britain as quickly as possible, and one of the fastest was *Madagascar*.

Owned by the famous London Blackwall shipping line, *Madagascar* was captained by Captain Fortescue Harris, an experienced seaman who knew the Australian run well. She had sailed out to Port Philip early in 1853 with the usual contingent of emigrants and by July lay under the Blue Peter, ready to return to England. As well as passengers, *Madagascar* carried 68,390 ounces of gold dust from the diggings, but just before Captain Harris ordered her to hoist her anchor, a loud hail came from the shore. Two detectives clambered on board with warrants to arrest two of the passengers. Captain Harris fumed while the detectives searched through the passenger's luggage.

'What have they done?'

'They're bushrangers. They robbed the McIvor Gold coach.'

Sure enough, the detectives found gold dust in the suspects' luggage, and Captain Harris had to wait while the trial took place. Found not guilty, the passengers seem to have returned on board and, a month late, *Madagascar* sailed for England. In common with so many ships at the time, she disappeared without trace, passengers, gold and ship, and that was the last anybody heard of *Madagascar*.

While some people claimed that she had sunk in a storm, others spoke of pirates and one or two, recalling the McIvor gold robbery, spoke darkly of a mutiny on board. It was not for many years that an old woman in New Zealand told the story about *Madagascar*'s last voyage.

Near to death, the old woman called for a clergyman and unburdened herself of her troubles.

She had been a nurse in her youth, and had sailed on board *Madagascar* when that ship left Melbourne for England. At first everything on the voyage had gone smoothly, but somewhere in the South Atlantic some of the crew and a number of passengers had mutinied. There had been terrible scenes in the ship as the mutineers hunted down and murdered the officers, then gradually captured all the other passengers. While the men, children and elderly women were locked up below, the young, good looking women were kept separate, in reasonable conditions. The old woman remembered their fear, for it was obvious why they were being kept alive.

After a few days the mutineers ordered all the boats lowered and forced the young women into them, together with the gold that they had torn from its hiding place. When mutineers and women were on board the heaving, jolting lifeboats the ship was fired. The lifeboats sailed away, leaving *Madagascar*, together with the other prisoners, a burning, smoking wreck.

However successful they were at murder, the mutineers were not seamen. As they rowed toward the coast of Brazil, the lifeboats capsized, until only one was left. Despite the desperate attempts of the men on board, even that boat sank in the surf of the South American coast, and the gold dust was lost before the few survivors crawled ashore.

There were no more dreams of luxurious living as the sun-scorched mutineers dragged themselves through the hostile land, hoping to find shelter and food. Yellow fever killed some, one went mad and a battered handful crawled into a tiny Brazilian village. Only two of the mutineers survived, and with them was their hostage, the one-time nurse. The nurse hung on as the men disappeared. One was lost forever, perhaps to die in the Brazilian rain forest, while the other fled to Frisco, where he became involved in a brawl and killed a man. He was hanged for murder.

When the minister heard the story he could do little but prepare the old woman for death. He knew that many questions remained. Why had she delayed telling her tale for so long? Perhaps she had been implicated in the mutiny? Or was her entire story only a fiction?

It was: this whole tale has been repeated by folklorists and at least one respected nautical historian, but it was completely false. There was a vessel named *Madagascar* and she did carry gold, but she vanished in 1853 without trace. All the rest is pure speculation: however it does make a good story.

Not so the tale of *Betsy Cairns*. She was no graceful clipper, but a Northumbrian collier, but her story could stand beside any in fiction or fact.

With proper care and maintenance, a wooden vessel could enjoy an almost indefinite life. Sometimes ships could undergo many transformations as they were used in different capacities. For instance a ship built for the timber trade from Quebec could be sold to a whaling company, then later work in the Baltic flax trade. However, few vessels can have experienced such a transformation as *Betsy Cairns*. When she came ashore at Tynemouth in February 1827, *Betsy Cairns* was working as a collier. She was eighty-three feet long, with a beam of twenty-three feet and, like most colliers, she was rigged as a brig. However, unlike other colliers, her mizzen yard was set for a lateen sail and her stem and stern were highly decorated with gilding and elaborate carving.

The colliers were essential to the economy of a nation that ran on coal. Coal fuelled the fires of a million homes, coal provided power for steam locomotives and steam engines, steam powered looms and steam powered factories. Without coal there was no steam, without steam there was no industrial revolution that kept Britain at the forefront of the world, and without colliers there was no coal.

At one time wreckers had plagued the coasts of England, but when *Betsy Cairns* came aground it was souvenir hunters who flocked to the ship. Rather than loot the cargo, they pulled the wreck to pieces in their search for a memento of a vessel which, they believed, had played an important part in the history of Britain. In the nineteenth century Geordie colliers had a reputation for toughness and seamanship second to none. Other seamen termed them 'Geordie Bears' because they were presumed to be uneducated, uncouth and rough. Scorning luxuries, the Geordies would climb aboard their vessel with a rope rather than a gang-plank; they ate the simplest of fare and often scorned book learning.

However they also knew the East Coast and the North Sea better than any other seamen in the world. Where other vessels would sign on anybody who could haul a rope, the Tyneside colliers accepted only 'half marrows' or men who had signed articles of apprenticeship. These men had to undergo seven often brutal years of training before they could be considered fit to sit the examination for an able seaman. The examination was an ordeal itself.

A committee of foremast hands would put the candidate through a thorough investigation. They would test him in every aspect of seamanship, from fitting a mast cover to putting a reef cringle into a sail, from gammoning a bowsprit to making a Turk's Head from a rope's end. If he failed in any aspect, he failed in all, and had to return to his lowly position as Ordinary Seaman for another period of learning before the committee would consider reconvening. Such hard schooling was necessary, for the North Sea was a vicious taskmaster. No quiet sea of predictable weather patterns and warm winds, the North Sea is shallow, dirty and treacherous. Squalls can kick up out of nothing, the coastline is close and dangerous, with few safe anchorages and a terrifying medley of shoals and rocks and ugly tides. If a man was not a seaman, he was a liability to his shipmates.

With men such as this, it was no wonder that vessels were kept afloat for generation after generation. But even so, *Betsy Cairns* was something special. There were rumours that she had been a West Indies sugar ship, one of the prestigious vessels that provided prosperity to Britain in the early days of Empire. There were also rumours that *Betsy Cairns* had an even more auspicious career. When she was wrecked, the 'Newcastle Courant' claimed that 'in 1688 the *Betsy Cairns* brought over to England William, Prince of Orange, and was then called the *Princess Mary*. For a number of years she was one of Queen Anne's royal yachts and at that time was considered a remarkably fast sailing vessel.'

At the time of her wreck in 1827, not only ardent royalists were interested in the career of *Betsy Cairns*. It was a period of much religious and political disputes, when Catholic Emancipation was seen as potentially damaging to the security of the state. Strangely, the supposed history of *Betsy Cairns* was tightly tied into the politico-religious debate. There was even a legend that there could be no emancipation as long as the ship had had allegedly carried King William was afloat. Pro and anti- emancipationists either hoped for her demise, or prayed for her continued survival.

There was a rumour, certainly apocryphal, that *Betsy Cairns* was deliberately sunk that February day in 1827. Not even the most fervent pro-emancipator was capable of whistling up a North Sea squall. Historians have disputed that *Betsy Cairns* could have carried King William, though possibly she was originally the royal yacht *Mary*, which transported Mary to England. However, only two years later, the Catholic Emancipation Act was passed, so perhaps there was a little magic in the ship after all.

Chapter Eight
Ships That Disappeared

Missing without trace; three words that every sea-farer and their dependants feared. Throughout history there have been so many ships that disappeared that it is impossible to calculate their number. In the days of sail, before radio or satellite, ships could be at sea for months without communication. With no fixed date of arrival there was no way of determining if a ship was lost, or merely delayed, until it was too late for the crew.

Delays by bad weather or bad luck were common. Storm, piracy, mutiny or the unknown; mariners could face any of these every voyage and although piracy diminished in the late 19th and during the 20th centuries, it was never completely eradicated and, indeed, has now returned on a scale unknown since the Royal Navy's anti-pirate patrols kept it well under control. Sir Walter Runciman in his book *Before the Mast – and After* mentions piracy: 'I had pretty narrow escapes in the Grecian Archipelago twice, and once in Tunis Bay.' He describes 'a black, snipish-looking vessel of the slave schooner type' and writes of an attempt to board as his vessel lay at anchor. This was in the latter half of the 19th century, at the height of Pax Britannica. Ships were always under threat of piracy among the islands of the East, the Philippines and Celebes being notorious, but there were always Chinese pirates ready to pounce as well. Piracy, however, was among the least of the mariner's concerns.

In 1886 Professor Francis Elgar addressed the Institute of Naval Architects on the subject of ship losses and stated that 264 British vessels of over 300 tons had sunk between 181 and 1883. These vessels were missing without trace. Eighty-six, he claimed, had carried coal and forty-four had carried grain. The professor linked the loss of the ships with the shift of cargo in bad weather.

'You can lose a ship anywhere and in so many ways' said Captain Learmont, a Solway mariner

'Fight the shore bastards and look after the ship all the time.'

He should have known. While sailing *Bengairn* from Newcastle to Valparaiso he ran into bad weather in the Tasman Sea. *Bengairn* heeled over. 'I thought I was getting a lesson on what happened to missing ships on that run' Learmont wrote.

The coal shifted, smashing through the main hatch and *Bengairn* was right over on her beam-ends. Only superb seamanship saved her. Learmont covered the gaping hatch with a sail, hacked free the topgallant mast, the royal mast and the connecting spars and spent days of anxiety and back breaking labour restoring the coal. *Bengairn* reached Sydney but rather than accept the dockyards quote for replacing masts and rigging, Learmont and his crew did the work themselves.

Sometimes ships had a lucky escape from the unknown. On 16th June 1899 Annan born Captain William Nelson, rounding the Cape of Good Hope in *Acamas* of Maryport, reported 'we had the startling experience of a thunderbolt dropping very close to the ship. At the same time a sudden gust of wind split the upper and lower topsails on both main and mizzen.'

If this 'thunderbolt or meteor' as he put it in the log, had landed on *Acamas*, what would have been her chances of survival? And who would know her fate?

This same Captain Nelson has a connection, albeit tenuous, with one of the major mysteries of the ocean, the loss of *Waratah*. In a later voyage of *Acamas*, Nelson carried seven apprentices. The voyage lasted well over two years, and five of the apprentices stayed the full term, being paid off in Glasgow. One of these, Apprentice Hemy, was promoted to third mate of SS *Commonwealth* and then to the steam liner *Waratah*.

After the hardship and strenuous work of a sailing ship, life on a steam passenger liner must have seemed much easier. But the sea was never a respecter of luxury. The Clydeside firm of Barclay, Curle and Co built *Waratah* in 1908. At 9339 tons she was the largest ship in the Blue Anchor Line and was intended to operate on the London to Sydney route. As the flower emblem of New South Wales, Waratah symbolised good luck.

With the veteran Captain Ilbury in command, *Waratah* successfully completed her maiden voyage to Sydney, via Cape Town and Durban, and returned to London. Her second outward trip seemed equally serene and on 7th July 1909 *Waratah* with 82 passengers and a mixed cargo of wheat, wool and frozen meat, left Sydney for Durban. There was a severe gale in mid ocean but Ilbury brought her safely through. The Chief Engineer seemed satisfied as her quadruple expansion engines thrust *Waratah* forward at a steady speed, despite her violent actions in the steep seas.

On arrival at Durban, Ilbury held a celebration for the return to London would be his last voyage. He was sixty-nine and due to retire. On the 26th July more passengers boarded, more cargo was loaded and the coalbunkers were refilled. At eight in the evening Captain Hugh Lindsay, the pilot came aboard and an hour later *Waratah* left harbour. It was a three-day journey to Cape Town and one day out *Waratah* met *Clan MacIntyre* of Glasgow. After an exchange of news *Clan MacIntyre* signalled 'Good-bye. Pleasant voyage' and *Waratah* replied 'Same to you. Good Bye.'

That was the last ever heard or seen of *Waratah*.

There had been a severe storm off Southeast Africa and many vessels scurried into the nearest ports for shelter, but *Waratah* was not among them. When she had not appeared by the beginning of August, a massive search began. The cruisers HMS *Forte*, HMS *Pandora*, HMS *Hermes* the tug *T.E.Fuller*, the Blue Anchor liner *Geelong* and the Union Castle Liner *Sabine* all scoured the sea for wreckage, the coast for stranded survivors, but found nothing.

A Board of Trade inquiry debated the disappearance. One theory said that her long promenade deck made *Waratah* unstable, liable to capsize. The builders denied this. The Durban pilot, Captain Lindsay, thought *Waratah* was unsuitable for the short, steep waves that rose off the Cape; he proposed that a huge wave had burst through her long forward hatch. Claude Sawyer, one of the passengers on her earlier voyage, claimed that *Waratah* had been so top heavy that her rolling had knocked people to the deck. After a succession of nightmares in which *Waratah* had capsized, Sawyer had cancelled his booking and saved his life.

Before leaving Durban, *Waratah* had loaded 1700 tons of coal, too much for the bunkers so the excess was piled on deck. It is possible that this coal had shifted during the storm. Some people claimed that Ilbury had also criticised *Waratah*'s handling. It was said that he had only withdrawn his complaints on being offered retirement. It was surely unlikely that a captain of thirty odd years' experience would sail in a ship he considered un-seaworthy, but it was easy to slander a missing man.

After the loss a clutch of stories came out; a minister meeting one of the dead passengers. 'But you were lost in the *Waratah*' said the minister.

'Yes, we turned over off East London.'

Or the woman who had intended to sail but had a premonition of disaster and so cancelled. All the same, and most unusually, she allowed her husband and two of her children to sail, and never saw them again.

So what happened? Did *Waratah* capsize in heavy seas? Was this Clyde built ship top heavy, or did her coal shift. The reason is possibly a combination of some or all of these. But *Waratah's* loss prompted the use of wireless on ships on this route and that in turn has probably saved hundreds of lives.

Nineteen years after the disappearance of *Waratah*, another Scottish built ship vanished mysteriously. This was *K'benhavn*, a 430-foot, five masted barque and the largest sailing ship ever built at Leith. In 1914 the East Asiatic Company of Copenhagen ordered her built by Ramage and Ferguson, but the First World War intervened. The Admiralty requisitioned this vessel. A second, identical ship was ordered and launched in the autumn of 1921. Primarily intended as a fast sailing ship, she also carried an auxiliary engine for entering port and in case of emergency. The East Asiatic Company meant her to be a training ship for cadets, while still working as a commercial cargo carrier. For a few years *K'benhavn* sailed successfully, then on December 14 1928 she left Buenos Aires for Melbourne with a crew of fifty-five mainly very young crewmen. She never made port.

As in the case of *Waratah* there was an extensive search but nothing was found. And then in 1995 when the visit of the Tall Ships Race to Leith brought back memories, came a possible solution. An article in Edinburgh's *Evening News* invited comments and one of the replies shed a little light. The island of Tristan da Cunha sits in the South Atlantic, remote from and ignored by the world until the volcanic eruption of 1961 brought evacuation and publicity. One of the islanders stated that the loss of *K'benhavn* was no mystery because he had watcher her go down off the north end of the island. Asked why he told nobody, the man said that back then it was not possible to just pick up a telephone.

It is possible that many other nautical mysteries could be solved by asking people on remote coasts, in isolated islands. The Inuit of northern Canada had stories of the loss of the Franklin Expedition of the 1840s, and stories about unknown white men of, perhaps, centuries earlier. Were there silent witnesses to the fate of Henry Hudson, set adrift in Hudson Bay with his son and seven men? Or to the voyage of the mate of the Greenock whaler *John?*

In 1829 while under the command of Captain Coombe, the crew of *John* mutinied off Lochryan. Next year, with the same captain and some of the same crew, *John* sailed for the whaling. Somewhere in the Arctic Captain Coombe died and there must have been another mutiny for the mate and a boat's crew were set adrift in the freezing sea and disappear from history. Like so many whalers that summer, *John* was sunk, taking her log with her. It is unlikely that the mate survived.

But some people did survive shipwrecks, and in the most unlikely of environments. In the early years of rounding the Cape of Good Hope, dozens of ships were lost, and there are strange tales of survivors turning up years later having been rescued and adopted by the local tribes. The South East Coast of Africa, the area in which *Waratah* presumably foundered, was notorious for such episodes. There was a clutch of wrecks in the early 1550s. *Saint Jerome* was lost with all hands north of the Mhlathuze mouth in Zululand. *San Joao*, carrying 610 people, was wrecked off today's Port

St John. Five hundred of those aboard made it to land. Twenty-five reached the nearest Portuguese settlement. Others, the sick, the injured, the despondent, were left at kraals the length of the journey. There was also *St Benedict*, which came ashore in Pondoland. Her survivors gave the name Rio de Medaos Do Ouro to the Tongaland Coast: *River of the Downs of Gold.*

During the next 50 years thousands of survivors staggered onto African soil, but only 500 arrived at what they termed civilisation. The remainder either died or joined the local peoples. One Englishman, shipwrecked in the closing years of the 17th century, met a Portuguese man who had survived a wreck more than forty years earlier. The Portuguese had been so integrated into the AmaPondo that he was content to remain an African tribesman. And why not? The African way of life was probably as good as or superior to, that of most Europeans. After the discipline and poor food on board ship, kraal life must have been an improvement.

One Scottish casualty on this coast was William Falconer, the Edinburgh born poet and seaman. He was wrecked twice in his career, once off the coast of Greece and the second and last time when HMS *Aurora* foundered off the Cape in 1769. Falconer is best remembered for his longest poem, ironically entitled *The Shipwreck*.

In 1790 an expedition searching for the survivors of an Indiaman lost eight years before came across a kraal on the Umgazana River. There were four hundred people here, all claiming descent from three European women who had been wrecked on the Natal coast many years before. Children played happily around the three grandmothers, or great grandmothers, who recalled only that they had been cast ashore as children. At one time there were so many wrecks around southeast Africa that the Bantu had a legend of a strange white race who lived on the bottom of the sea. Rather than UFOs, here were UMPs, Unidentified Marine People, and unnumbered Africans were unasked witnesses to tragedy.

The Scottish coast has also seen its share of shipping losses and mysteries. Fifty yards off Camachair in Hirta, the main island of the St Kilda group; Mina Stac protrudes from the sea. At one time, according to legend, there was a natural archway between this stack and the cliffs of Hirta. During the autumnal storms of 1588 one of the fleeing ships of the Spanish Armada was driven toward the island. Either the ferocity of the storm hid the nature of the arch, or the captain attempted to squeeze his ship underneath, but his topmast struck the rock above. The resulting rock fall resulted in hundreds of tons of jagged stone not only sinking the ship but also isolating the stack. The legend does not mention survivors. It is doubtful if the Spanish government asked the people of St Kilda if they knew anything about a missing ship.

Although this particular wreck may be apocryphal, at least four Spanish vessels did founder off the Scottish coast; the most famous of these lies in Tobermory Bay. This was the transport *San Juan de Sicilia*, and there are dark stories of Spanish soldiers being used as mercenaries by MacLean of Duart, and of a lone clansman blowing up the ship.

Another, just north of Collieston in St Catherine's Dub was probably sunk in the early 1590s. A third, *Barea Amburg*, went down off Fair Isle, while

El Gran Griffon was driven onto the Fair Isle cliffs in September 1588. This was neither the first nor the last wreck on Fair Isle. The earliest known was in 900 AD when a Viking long ship came to grief; the last ... will there ever be a last shipwreck?

Those Spaniards were the lucky ones. More common was the end of the Robert Steele built, Scottish crewed *Romsdal.* This was a fine ship, used for both the jute trade and the North Pacific grain trade. No slouch, she once crossed from Tail of the Bank to Montreal and back to Liverpool in 37 days and she sailed from Dundee to Rangoon in 97 days – excellent times. Under Captain Whyte she was happy, with Mrs Whyte adding the family touch which the best seagoing women could. On October 31 1891, in company with *County of Selkirk, Romsdal* left Chittagong with a cargo of jute. Within two days she was battling a cyclone. Only wreckage of *Romsdal* was ever found although *County of Selkirk* better positioned when the storm hit, survived. There was no fault with *Romsdal,* her captain or her crew, but the sea could be hard on sailing ships. Among the most beautiful of creations, they could also be killers.

Lost without trace.

Chapter Nine
Severed Heads and Bare Breasted Women

In times past, many seamen believed that their vessels had an individual character. There were stories of ships that could navigate their own passage across the Atlantic, and of ships that could find their own familiar berth even on the foggiest of days. One way of expressing this individuality was through a figurehead. One of the most famous figureheads is surely that of *Cutty Sark*, where a buxom woman thrusts herself before the ship, wearing only the cutty sark, or short shirt that Burns featured in his poem.

Cutty Sark, however, was not unique. In the nineteenth century it was not uncommon for ships to have a bare breasted woman as figurehead. There was a prevailing superstition among seamen that such a sight would calm down the wrath of the sea and ensure a smooth passage. As *Cutty Sark* is one of the few clipper ships to have survived from that great age of sail, perhaps there is no reason to scoff. Ship's companies tended to believe that their figurehead was a good luck charm and kept it in good repair, with some receiving scores of coats of paint as protection against the weather. Any damage to a figurehead meant a corresponding lowering of morale in the ship, but sometimes retaining a figurehead could be a liability.

During the American War of Independence, the Royal Navy and British privateers decimated American shipping. One of the vessels captured was the United States privateer *Truelove*, which the British used as a whaling ship. Sailing from Hull, *Truelove* was an extremely successful whale hunter, but she had one drawback; her figurehead attracted ice. Whaling ships worked in the worst environment in the world, right on, or often beyond, the edge of the Arctic ice. They acted as mother ships while the small whale boats rowed or sailed out to hunt for the whales. Every year there were casualties, with ships being punctured or crushed by the ice, and men suffering from disease or frostbite. The whalers were known as Greenlandmen, and they did not need an additional hazard. So when it was realised that the figurehead was gathering so much ice that it pulled *Truelove* down by the head, it had to go. *Truelove* sailed, shorn of part of her identity, for many more years.

Despite the dangers, other whaling vessels displayed a figurehead. There was *Chieftain* of Dundee, who boasted the figurehead of a Highland warrior. She also had a chequered history, losing many of her crew when they were out sealing in a thick Greenland fog, to accompanying rumours of cannibalism. There was also *Arctic*, which Alexander Stephen built as late as 1875. One of the few whaling vessels to have a public house named in her honour, *Arctic* was 828 tons in gross weight and over 200 feet long. Her figurehead was distinctive too, an Inuit holding a lance who guided *Arctic* into becoming one of the most celebrated of the entire Dundee fleet.

Many maritime peoples have used figureheads on ships. The origins are mysterious, but possibly contained both religious symbolism and a person-ification of the ship. One theory suggests that very early mariners believed that the sea was divine, and offered a human sacrifice when they launched a new ship. There are tales of early ships being physically launched across a human body so that the blood helped smooth her passage to the sea. Other legends say that a human was beheaded and the head placed on the bow of the boat, where the Sea God could not fail to see it. However, as more ships were built, it became difficult to find enough sacrifices, so somebody fashioned a crude head out of wood, or perhaps a mop of rope. In time this device became common, and was ac-cepted as the figurehead of the boat. There are, of course, many other theories.

Like so many things nautical, figureheads were known in the ancient Mediterranean, where Egyp-tian vessels carried carvings of holy birds on the prow. It is possible that Egyptian figureheads were detachable, to be changed depending on the altered use of the vessel. The insignia on the poop of these heavily curved craft certainly was

That figureheads were regarded as more than merely ornamental is proved by the Phoenicians, those functional mariners, traders and slavers of the Levant. Their black ships were the epitome of professionalism, but carried the figureheads of a horse's head. Religion, superstition and seamanship have always been very closely intertwined. Fighting Greek ships boasted the head of a boar, while the Romans thought that nothing but a carved centurion could demonstrate the power of their ships.

The oldest surviving figurehead is that of a Greek trireme, the winged Victory of Samothrace that now graces the Louvre. Demetrius, a soldier who fought for the great Alexander, set up this creation at Samothrace in 306 BC, and if it may never have decorated the prow of a ship, it is surely a representation of others that did. This figurehead proclaims that Alexander's Macedonians were masters of the sea as well as of the land, much as the representation of Britannia shouted triumph, two thousand years and more in the future.

While legend claims that the Vikings often decorated the prow of their long ships with the heads of their victims, more sober history credits Norse ships with serpents, dolphins or bulls. However, Sweyn Forkbeard of Denmark sailed a unique dragonship, with the stern of the vessel decorated as the creature's tail and a dragon's head as the figurehead. The Normans, lineal descendants of the Vikings, also used figureheads. When William the Conqueror crossed the Channel in 1066, his ship had a lion's head as figurehead.

While most maritime nations could exchange ideas and techniques, the people of the Furthest East seem to have gone their own way in many things: neither the Japanese nor the Chinese used figureheads on their vessels. The Chinese contented themselves with an eye, so that the ship could find her own way. Further east still, the war canoes of the Maori had some amazingly elaborate carvings. In early mediaeval Europe, some seamen would refuse to sail unless the ship bore a figurehead that could scare away demons. By that time the style for European figureheads had rigid-ified into either a dragon or a large fish, whose protuberant tongue doubled as a ram.

The first recorded British figurehead seems to have been that of *Trinity Royal* in 1416, which car-ried the royal English leopard, crowned with cop-per, on her beak-head. By the sixteenth century, figureheads on Scottish or English ships were of-ten related to the name of the vessel. For instance the Scottish warship *Unicorn* had a unicorn figure-head; there is a nineteenth century warship of that name in Victoria dock, Dundee, with a fine uni-corn figurehead. Nevertheless, there seemed no fixed rule, for the sixteenth century English vessel *Mary Rose* also had a unicorn figurehead.

In the seventeenth and eighteenth century, naval decoration reached a peak, with each royal vessel vying in elaboration with the next. *Sovereign of the Seas*, later renamed *Sovereign* and *Royal Sovereign*, was a very busy vessel. In her sixty-year career she took part in no less than six ma-jor fleet actions. Her figurehead was a splendid representation of historical propaganda, showing a mounted King Edgar trampling down the seven kings that English documents claim rowed his royal barge.

While British battleships contented themselves with figureheads of royalty, the French were supreme in the art of elaboration. The French flagship *Le Roi Soleil* carried a figurehead of a mermaid, while another three-decked battleship had a female in flowing robes, with a trumpet in one hand, a flag in the other, standing on a carpet of oak leaves. Smaller European warships in the seventeenth century often carried a lion rampant figurehead, whatever their nationality. The shape and angle, or 'sweep of the lion' followed fixed rules that shipbuilders had to obey. In 1703, the English Admiralty ordered that the lion should be the figurehead for every royal warship below the first rate.

Standardisation continued in the eighteenth century, when many ships carried a figurehead of a Roman soldier. Classical education in public schools had turned the nautical wheel full circle as *Temeraire, Warrior, Royal George* and *Kent* fought behind the same figure that had led the Roman vessels two thousand years previously. To continue the classical theme, Neptune, the Roman sea god, also acted as figurehead, while the one-eyed Cyclops stared out from the beak of *Polyhemus*. However, a dragon-slaying St George added a touch of mediaeval Christianity to other vessels.

Interestingly it was the nineteenth century that figureheads achieved their full potential. While some harked back to the past, such as *Royal Adelaide*, which had a double life size carving of the queen, other vessels had more individuality. The topsail schooner *Devil* carried Lucifer on her bow, and her reputation supported her name. Black painted, she hailed from Preston and crossed the Atlantic at a devilishly fast speed, despite the bad weather that seemed to dog her raking hull. Rumour said that *Devil* was sailing along the West African Coast when her crew sickened with fever. With only her figurehead to guide her, *Devil* disappeared forever. *Styx* was another diabolical vessel, with a naked devil, painted bitter brown, as a figurehead.

Not all figureheads were so dramatic, however. In 1830 the East Indiaman *Thames* had the figure of Father Thames complete with trident, a London version of Neptune.

Some colourful stories were spun around the nineteenth century figureheads. One of the most interesting concerned *Java*, which was built in Calcutta in 1813. *Java's* figurehead was a representation of a naked woman with her hands pressed together in prayer. According to the story, the man who ordered her built also handed her to an officer of the Honourable East India Company. The builder was a British merchant who traded along the coasts of the East, often taking his wife and family with him. These coasts were dangerous in the early Nineteenth century, with various types of pirate and broken men waiting to attack merchant vessels. While the merchant was away, a group of savages snatched his daughter and disappeared into the wilds of the jungle.

The merchant was distraught, but he was a man of trade, not a man of war. Luckily, a British officer heard about the kidnapping and gathered together a force of adventurers. They followed the trail of the missing girl, hacking through dense jungle until they located the camp of the kidnappers. There was a brief skirmish, with pistols popping and swords flickering, and the officer found the merchant's daughter, naked and afraid but unhurt, in the middle of the camp. Unfortunately, the story seems to be apocryphal, but it does give some colour to the figurehead.

In 1833, the government ended the East India Company's exclusive charter to trade with India. Green and Wigram's shipbuilding yard at Blackwall in London immediately stepped into the vacancy and built a number of vessels for the Indian trade. These ships were known as Blackwall frigates, mainly because they were faster than the bulky East Indiamen. *Seringapatam* was the first Blackwall frigate. Built in 1837, she weighed 818 tons and set up a new speed record between London and Bombay.

Known as 'Old Seringy', *Seringapatam* was often remembered for another of her attributes. Her figurehead represented Tipoo Sahib, complete with a drawn scimitar. Tipoo Sahib or Tipu Sultan was one of the East India Company's most formidable enemies. When his father, Hyder Ali was Sultan of Mysore, Tipu defeated three successive British armies, and captured many British soldiers including the redoubtable Captain David Baird, then became sultan himself. Tipu kept Baird a prisoner for four harrowing years, but even after the peace, he remained a major player in the politics of Southern India.

Inevitably, another war began and David Baird, now a Major-General, led the army that captured Tipu's capital of Seringapatam. It was a good story, and Tipu had been a worthwhile enemy, so there was no shame in naming a ship in his honour. Certainly the people of southern India had never forgotten their Sultan, and whenever *Seringapatam* sailed up the Calcutta River, they salaamed and saluted the figurehead. A great warrior, Tipu also proved a fine figurehead, for he led *Seringapatam* safely past icebergs in 1841 and survived a great cyclone of 1851.

The 19th century was prodigal with the lives of ships and men. Every year, scores of ships would sink, often without trace, leaving only another mystery of the sea. However, there were occasions when the figurehead of a lost ship would float ashore, carrying a mute tale of death and loss and sorrow. In 1869 *Blue Jacket* caught fire off the Falkland Islands in the South Atlantic. Her crew abandoned her, taking to the boats, and thought they would hear no more of their ship. However, in December 1871, two years and nine months later, the sea washed the figurehead of Blue Jacket onto Rottnest Island, Western Australia, thousands of miles away. She had made her last landfall.

Although figureheads were usually based on historical, mythical or literary personalities, there were occasions when a living woman was so honoured. In the nineteenth century Dundee was a very busy port, with whaling ships sailing to the Arctic, brigs bound for the Baltic and the great jute clippers sailing to Bengal and back. The Cox family owned what was probably the largest jute factory in the world, with a workforce of 5000 at its Lochee mill, a private railway and a majority share holding in a fleet of clipper ships. This fleet was commonly known as the Dundee Clipper line. Around 1870 one of the Dundee clippers was named *Duntrune*, in honours of the house of Mrs Clementena Graham of Duntrune, who was a descendant of Graham of Claverhouse, who was better known as 'Bluidy Claver'se' or 'Bonnie Dundee', depending whether the speaker was a Jacobite or a Covenanter. Mrs Graham was also a friend of Admiral Duncan, victor of the Battle of Camperdown, and a notable author who wrote *Mystification*. She also named *Duntrune*, launched her and, at the age of 95, modelled the figurehead. It is unlikely there are many people who could match that!

Today there are few, if any figureheads on commercial ships, but people are still interested in these unwieldy, unseamanlike objects that added to the weight of the ship. They were part of life for tens of thousands of seamen over thousands of years, a sort of ship borne talisman, yet it is unlikely that anybody could explain their attraction. Perhaps figureheads did indeed impart personality to the ships, or perhaps there was something more, something that only seamen on long, lonely voyages, could understand. To the landsman, figureheads would always appear strange.

Chapter Ten
Creatures of the Deep

From the time that mariners first pushed out beyond the horizon, there have been tales of strange creatures that live in the sea. Sometimes the tales were of monsters, at other times they were of selkies or seal-people, but often they were of mermaids. Many mariners spoke of these creatures, with the top half of a human and the lower half of a fish, but modern science has dismissed the tales as delusion, fiction or downright lies. Modern writers speak of dugongs or manatees, the gentle creatures that graze along the sea bed near the coasts, but these creatures bear only a superficial resemblance to humans. However sex-starved a seaman after a long voyage, he was unlikely to mistake an ugly, whiskered, broad faced dugong for the silky beauty of a mermaid.

In 1730, Louis Renard, a British spy in the Netherlands published a book showing the sea creatures that were supposed to exist in the great Southern Sea. One of the more exotic was a mermaid with a rather woebegone expression on her face and a short note about her lifestyle. Apparently this creature 'lived on shore in a tub for four days and seven hours. It occasionally uttered cries like that of a mouse.' Such misleading information was not unusual in an age which favoured phrases such as 'here be dragons' rather than geographical knowledge to fill in the blank spaces in maps, but did bring public attention to ponder on the possible existence of mermaids.

Spread over centuries and from seas and coasts across half the world, the accounts still have the ability to mystify. What is interesting is the matter-of-fact manner in which sightings are entered in the ship's log. The master frequently put down the bare facts, with no attempt at justification or judgement. He simply wrote what was seen. In 1607, Henry Hudson, an English explorer of the Arctic, wrote that one his men saw a 'mermaid, long haired, white and human breasted at one end, and mackerel speckled at the other.'

There have never been reports of the tropical dugongs in the cold waters off Spitsbergen, while Hudson's journal is filled with sightings such as:

'July 9. Today we were in among islands of ice, where we saw many seals'

'June 29. There were many walruses in the sea near us.'

These seamen were well aware of the difference between a seal and a mermaid. They were also aware that mermaids were not common. In 1610 Richard Whitbourne was standing by the water in Saint John's in Newfoundland, when he saw a 'strange Creature.' He said that the animal 'come swimming toward me, looking cheerefully, as it had been a woman... it seemed to be so beautifull, and in those parts so well proportioned...' Joined by a companion, Whitbourne watched the creature swim nearby, 'whereby I beheld the shoulders and back downe to the middle, to be as square, white and smooth as the back of a man, and from the middle to the hinder part, pointing in proportion.'

Other men, including Whitbourne's servant William Hawkridge, watched as the creature came close and 'put both his hands upon the side of the Boate...whereas they were afraid; and one of them strooke it a full blow on the head; whereas it fell off.' At sight of the creature, two 'other Boates...for feare fled to land.' Whitbourne concluded, 'this (I suppose) was a Mermaide.'

Mermaids seemed to have a vast geographical spread. On the 11th November 1602, the Honourable East India Company's ship *Ascension* reported seeing a pair of 'marmaides.' The report, somewhat laconic, said 'their hinde parts were divided into two legges', while the ship's husband believed that they were husband and wife 'because the moste of one of their heads was longer than the other.' Rather than be astonished at the sight, the report continued 'they say they are signes of bad weather, and so we found it.' That report suggests that the possibility of bad weather was more important than the sighting of mermaids for themselves.

Just a century later, the English vessel *Worcester* of 160 tons and 16 guns was 'just without Delagoa

River's mouth' when the crew saw a mermaid. They reported that 'a creature appeared to them out of the water three times successively, within about 10 yards of the boat, continuing some time out of the water at each of its appearances, staring the men in the face, and then dived under water. It lifted itself out of the water to the waist, was of the bigness of a large woman of a tawny complexion, with dark brown hair on the head hanging over the shoulders, and stared from some time at each of its appearances.'

There seems to be no specific time, year or place for seeing mermaids. On the 26th August 1912 Joao Pirea of the Cape Verde Islands, while serving on the United States whaling brig *Daisy* saw what he called a sereia or mermaid. He reported it quite laconically, as if there was nothing really unusual about the sight.

While most pieces of sea folklore are confined to seamen, land based people also occasionally met mermaids. The Scottish coast in particular seemed to hold a fascination for these elusive creatures, which have a longer history than may be supposed. Mary Queen of Scots was often depicted as a mermaid, which was supposed to be an immoral creature, while serious minded clerics held long discussions as to whether mermaids had souls. In November 1811 there was a formal tribunal in Campbeltown to investigate local sightings of a mermaid.

An eight year old child named Catherine Loynachan had seen the creature, which she had believed to be a boy from a shipwreck. She reported that the creature had rubbed its breast with one hand before it slipped into the water and swam away. A local girl, Catherine would know all about sea creatures that came onto the Kintyre peninsula, and her evidence was backed by a mature man, John McIsaac, who saw a creature lying on a rock. The top half was white and shaped like a human body, 'and the other half, toward the tail, of a brindled or reddish grey colour, apparently covered with scales, but the extremity of the tail itself was of a greenish red shining colour.'

Other Scottish sightings include a mermaid on a rock in Caithness, another in the Isle of Muck and one in Sandwood Bay, Sutherland in 1900. In January 1832 the 'Inverness Advertiser' gave a relatively detailed report of a mermaid sighting. The newspaper said that the crew of a boat from Ullapool 'discovered a figure, apparently that of a man…engaged in fishing…to their utter amazement [the crew] found it to be partly the likeness of a human being, of which the uppermost half resembled a female and was white as snow, and the other half was of a sky blue colour and had fins and a tail like a fish. The monster was very tame and had soft rolling eyes.'

Were these instances truth or fiction? These examples are only samples from a vast amount of sightings over many centuries, and in many seas. It is unlikely that so many people would have simply made up their stories, particularly as they would expect ridicule from their peers. Perhaps they were mistaken, or did, in fact, see a seal or some other marine creature. However, experienced seamen would be well aware of the difference between a seal, or a dugong, or an otter, and an unknown creature. Bering, for instance, saw an unusual creature on August 10th 1741 while he was sailing off Alaska. Naming the creature a 'sea-ape', Bering described it as having a head like a dog with erect and pointed ears, large eyes, thick body hair and long whiskers. It had no forefeet, but a divided flipper or tail. This creature was later identified as a bachelor fur-seal. To date, nobody has identified an animal that answers the descriptions of a mermaid.

Perhaps then, there are still some unknown creatures in the sea, waiting to be discovered. Perhaps the aggression shown to them by past seamen have driven them away until humanity is more civilised.

So why are mermaids not seen today? Perhaps motor engines scare them, or the speed of modern vessels precludes such sightings. It is intriguing to think that there might be some race of animals in the sea that resemble us in part, but until such an animal is identified on film, mermaids are destined to remain just another mystery of the sea.

The albatross is another creature that has entered the realm of nautical mythology, but there is no doubt about its reality. It was Samuel Taylor Coleridge in his 1798 poem, 'Rime of the Ancient Mariner' who popularised the albatross in the minds of the literate. Seamen, however, had long regarded this massive bird, with its fifteen foot wingspan, with something like awe. The albatross is a native of the southern hemisphere and often follows a ship for weeks at a time, remaining on station with its wing tips erect and its eyes constantly questing.

British seamen once believed that the albatross is the soul of a seaman in a state of bliss, while Wilson's Petrel contains the black soul of a landsman, condemned forever to wander the oceans of the world. While 18th century seamen would not (in theory anyway) hurt an albatross, those of the 19th century, much more familiar with Cape Horn, had fewer scruples. The wings and head made popular decorations; the down stuffed cushions and the wing bones were used as paper knives. The lower wing bones were useful pipe stems and the feet used for tobacco pouches. The beak was a coat hanger and if the bird was young and tender, it could also be eaten.

Although Coleridge popularised the myth of the albatross, it was an earlier writer of that century who first wrote of it. Captain George Shelvocke was an English Privateer born in Shropshire but spent most of his life ashore in London. He commanded the 22-gun *Speedwell and* in 1726 he wrote a book about his exploits, in which he spoke about Hatley shooting the albatross. The book is hard to find but has an elegant and catchy title:

A Voyage around the world, by way of the great south sea: performed in a private expedition during the war, which broke out with Spain, in the year 1718

No doubt Coleridge was familiar with this book but William Wordsworth also claimed to have had some input into the Navigator, claiming that in 1798 he, his sister and Coleridge planned the 'Ancient Mariner' which was 'founded on a dream, as Mr Coleridge said, of his friend Mr Cruickshank. Much the greatest part of the story was Mr Coleridge's invention; but certain parts I myself suggested: - for example some crime was to be committed which should bring upon the old Navigator, as Coleridge afterwards delighted to call him, the spectral persecution, as a consequence of that crime, and his own wanderings. I had been reading in *Shelvock's Voyages* a day or two before that while doubling Cape Horn they frequently saw Albatrosses in that latitude..."'Suppose," said I. "you represent him as having killed one of these birds on entering the South Sea, and that the tutelary Spirits of those regions take upon them to avenge the crime..." I also suggested the navigation of the ship by the dead men...'

Perhaps it is because of their mobile eyes that the albatross was reckoned a special bird. Generations of seamen believed that the souls of dead seafarers enter into an albatross, so it was unlucky to shoot such a creature. The newly homeless ghost of the seaman would haunt the killer as long as he was afloat. Knut Weibest in his *Deep Sea Sailors* recounted the story of a seaman who looked into the eyes of an albatross off Cape Horn and recognised them as the eyes of a shipmate who had drowned in the North Sea.

In 1912 a passenger on the United States whaler *Daisy* remarked that the captain was unhappy because he had shot several albatrosses. Apparently it was perfectly acceptable to catch an albatross on a bent nail or thump one with a belaying pin, but shooting them was beyond the pale.

It is suspected that a single incident created this perception that albatrosses resented being shot. Simon Hatley was third mate of *Duchess* during Commodore Rogers' daring circumnavigation in 1708. Given command of a Spanish prize, Hatley promptly disappeared, despite an extensive search by other vessels of Rogers' squadron. Short of water, he had headed for South America, only for the Spaniards to capture him. Incarcerated in a Lima dungeon, Hatley did not get home to England until after the treaty of Utrecht in 1713, yet he still returned to the sea. It was while attempting the Horn in 1719 that a succession of storms reawakened the melancholic thoughts of the Spanish dungeon, and Hatley began to hate the 'disconsolate black albatross' that hovered around the masthead. Lifting his pistol, she shot it dead, which was quite a feat given the shifting deck of a Cape Horner and the inaccuracy of an early eighteenth century firearm.

Eighty years later, Coleridge immortalised the deed, if not the mariner:

'God save thee, ancient Mariner
from the fields, that plague thee thus!

Why look'st thou so? With my crossbow
I shot the Albatross.'

Of course, these legends all belong to the dim past. Once the era of sail had past, seamen lost their superstitious beliefs. Or perhaps not. As recently as 1959, the ship *Calpean Star* sailed from the Antarctic to Germany, but put into Liverpool with engine trouble. Many of the crew immediately scrambled ashore, complaining that the ship had a cargo of trouble. They blamed everything on the albatross that they were carrying to a German zoo. Unable to find a replacement crew, the ship's master was pleased when the albatross died, along with the misfortunes of the voyage.

Other sea birds are also special to seamen. For instance Wilson's Petrel is said to be the damned soul of a landsman, while the prion was known as the ice bird, as it was always present when ice was nearby. The prion, which skims the tops of waves and flies deep in their troughs, was also known as the whalebird, as was the cape pigeon. Both were seen when whales were nearby. None of these birds, however, had the enduring charisma of the albatross. Yet, even with all the stories, it was often remarked that no pure white albatross ever followed a British ship. In the long night watches in the Doldrums, while the ship drifted over azure seas and the sails hung limp beneath a broiling sun, seamen debated the mystery of the wandering albatross.

Some said that the pure white birds were the fully mature adults, which were too delicate to stand the biting cold of the far south. Others had a more prosaic answer. Agreeing that the pure white birds were adults, they added that they had learned enough wisdom never to know that they would find little food thrown overboard from a ship with a penny pinching British purser on board.

Other birds were also important to the old time mariners. Anne Frazer, a passenger on a voyage between London and the Falkland Islands in 1880 mentioned Mother Carey's Chickens 'sailors do not like to kill them as they are said to be sent by the sailor's wives and sweethearts to cheer them on their long way.'

Yet despite the favour with which seamen regarded the albatross, they were just birds, as fickle as any other creature. In November 1862 the ship *Alfre*, was outward bound to Australia when a midshipman name Reynolds fell overboard from the foc'sle head. The ship was travelling at nine knots before a westerly wind and the master ordered the flying jib, royals and foretopgallant sails to be taken in, while the mainyard was backed even as both lifeboats were launched. The men pulled at the oars, but as they closed they saw the boy struggling in the water with a cloud of mollyhawks and albatrosses attacking him. Unable to cope with both the sea and the birds, Midshipman Reynolds died before he was rescued.

Midshipman Reynolds was unlucky, but other mariners could experience misfortune with sea creatures and survive. The story of Jonah is well known, and many people sneer at the possibility that a whale, or any other marine animal, could swallow a man. Nevertheless, there is a story that suggests that such a thing might just happen. In 1891 the United States whaler *Star of the East* was working off the Falkland Islands in the South Atlantic when a seaman named James Bartley fell overboard. Such things often happened at sea, and after the perfunctory search, Bartley was given up for dead.

Star of the East killed a sperm whale that same day, and the crew dragged the kill close alongside. They stripped it of the blubber that would be transformed into oil for heating, lighting and industry and then began the search for ambergris. This ash-grey, high scented waxy substance was secreted from the intestines of sperm whales and was often found floating in the sea or on tropical coasts. Because of its strong scent, ambergris was extensively used in the manufacture of perfume.

As they were rummaging through the intestines of the dead whale, the men realised that the creature still seemed to be moving. Some part of the animal was stirring, writhing around. At first there was some superstitious fear, and then gradually the whalers thought that perhaps a sea creature was still alive in the stomach. Carefully, they cut through to the thing, and were shocked to find their late ship mate. James Bartley, doubled up, unconscious and smeared with slime, was within the stomach of the whale.

For two weeks, Bartley lay delirious in his bunk as his shipmates cared for him as best they could. Then he gradually recovered consciousness and told his story. He said that he had been drowning when he fell overboard, then he seemed to enter a warm, moving passage. After a time, he knew that he was in the stomach of the whale. Bartley claimed that the heat had been terrible, but enough air seeped through to keep him alive. However, the acids of the whale's stomach had taken their effect, and Bartley's skin remained a bleached white for the remainder of his life. Was this strange tale true or false?

Whales, of course, were never merely the supine victims of whaling ships. They could strike back when necessary, which helps to explain the motto of American whalers, 'a dead whale or a stove boat.' Often the contest between men in a small whaling boat and their prey was not totally unequal as the whale could be up to four times the length of the boat. Another saying was 'beware of a sperm's jaw and a right whale's fluke.' The Arctic seamen were rightly nervous of the lashing flukes of a whale, which could upend a whaleboat in an instant, sending the crew into bitter water where survival was only a matter of minutes.

While Arctic whalers were in peril from the flukes of the Greenland Right Whales that they hunted from their small boats, the great sperm whales were fully capable of destroying a ship. In 1819 a sperm whale rammed the Nantucket whaling ship *Essex*, with the force of the impact damaging Essex so she began to sink. The crew took to the boats, and when the British brig *India* and the whaler *Dauphin* rescued the survivors some 90 days later, there were tales of death by starvation and cannibalism.

The tale of the United States whaler *Exeter* is nearly as well known as the story of Jonah, but she was not alone. On May 19 1874 the barque *Minstrel King* of Swansea was in latitude 54 degrees south, longitude 85 west in the Southern Ocean, enjoying strong breezes and a calm sea.

Shortly after two in the afternoon the lookout noticed a large sperm whale astern of the ship, and the crew watched as the whale swam after *Minstrel King* and rammed her with some force. The whale repeated the attack on a number of occasions, before swimming directly underneath the hull. As the crew watched in wonderment, the whale raised its head, lifting the after end of the ship between twelve and eighteen inches out of the water, starting the steering gear and knocking two men to the deck.

George Jameson the master calculated that the whale was between 130 and 140 feet in length; *Minstrel King* was 150 feet long and when alongside the whale extended from the after pumpkin to before the cathead. When the whale began to strike at the stern with its tail, the master called all hands on deck, expecting that the rudder would be unshipped and the sternpost damaged, but *Minstrel King* was a tough vessel and there was no external damage. All the same, he thought it best to scare the whale away, so used the ship's bell, foghorn and a selection of tin drums to make as much noise as possible, which seemed effective as the animal retreated.

Herman Melville was correct with the idea of Moby Dick as sperm whales could be dangerous animals, and had a tendency to turn on their back, open their mouth and keep the double row of teeth threatening the fragile whale boat beneath. The threat of having the boat bitten in half was sometimes enough to force the crew to leap overboard, while on one occasion in 1836 an American whaling boat was actually chewed in half. Naturally the whaling men named the most aggressive of these animals, with one particularly well known whale christened New Zealand Tom. His white hump may have echoes of Moby Dick.

With folklore not being an exact science, it is possible that New Zealand Tom and Old Tom was the same animal, recorded in different ways, but Old Tom appeared regularly each winter from around 1843 until 1930 and was anything but a man killer. Old Tom worked off Twofold Bay in New South Wales, and helped the whaling men of the village of Eden. When they found a victim, Old Tom and a band of killer whale followers grabbed the tail of the prey, and sometimes leaped onto the blowhole until it rolled onto the surface. The whaling men lanced the animal to death, and Old Tom got the tongue and lips with the humans grabbing the rest. This partnership continued until

Old Tom died, whereupon the other killer whales disappeared.

Overall, there are many tales of the animals that live in the sea, but none stranger than that of the sea monsters.

Chapter Eleven
Sea Monsters

The sea held other monsters other than whales. The 19th century seemed to be a boom time for reporting the unusual, perhaps because there were more vessels travelling to more destinations, or because of the expansion of a popular press hungry for anecdotal news to feed the masses.

For example there was the brig *Trim*, Captain Cleveland on passage from Gibraltar to Alexandria on 25 October 1815. In latitude 51, longitude 20 the lookout saw what he thought was a sea serpent about 25 feet away from the vessel. The lookout was so surprised that he called the captain. The captain tacked the ship, and with the wind W. S. W. and very light he thought it safe to lower a boat with the mate and two men on board and orders to row closer to see exactly what they had seen.

The mate took the boat right over the spot where they had seen the serpent. They looked over the side; the creature was about four feet under the surface of the water. It was coiled up with its head on top of the coil. The mate said that the head was about 14 inches long and pointed, with pointed tusks that appeared about three or four inches in length. The body, he thought, was about three and a half feet in circumference, crimson and tapered as it stretched toward the tail.

However the smack of the oars startled the creature and it rose through the water, thrusting its head above the water as if it was about to attack the men in the boat. As the creature was around 35 feet long, the mate thought it prudent to withdraw to Trim, and by the time they got on board, the serpent had vanished.

The Mediterranean was busy with serpents that decade. In December 1811 H.M. brig *Philomel* anchored in the Bay of Algiers, about three miles east of the city. They had orders to sound and chart the bay; possibly the Admiralty had plans for future operations against the slavery in the city, as indeed happened once the Napoleonic War was won. While they were there, one of their cables snagged and parted in nine fathoms of water. One of the seamen had been fishing from the poop and said he saw 'the devil in the shape of a serpent' cut the cable and it was beside the ship now. A civilian named Mitford was in the ship and saw four creatures about thirty feet in length, wriggling and moving around in the water. He described them as dark brown with a 'silvery tinge on the belly' and about the circumference of a 'stout man's thigh.'

Even with these creatures in the water, the hands swam in the sea without molestation or fear. They also tried to catch them with shark hooks, with no success at all. The local people said they were common thereabouts and believed that if they ever left, so would the fish.

That decade was also rife with sightings of sea serpents off the Atlantic coast of North America. In 1817 one or more were seen off Cape Ann and Kettle Island, New England. In October a boat and a sloop set off from Marblehead to try and kill the animal, but as soon as they left harbour the weather turned against them and they were forced to anchor in the outer harbour. The following year Jonathan Webber and Richard Hamilton of Portland, Maine were rowing a small boat to the fishing ground near Crouch Island Point when they came across what they also thought was a sea serpent. They said it was in three coils and about twenty feet long with protuberances on its back.

There were many other sightings of strange or unidentified marine animals throughout the 19th century. In June 17 1826 Captain Henry Holridge was crossing from Liverpool to New York in the emigrant ship *Silas Richards* when in latitude 41 degrees 3 minutes, longitude 67. 32, an unknown but huge creature surfaced not far from their ship.

Holridge, his crew and the passengers all lined the rails of the packet ship and stared. It was eight minutes before the creature slid away. The part of the creature they could see was around sixty feet in length, with perhaps another ten feet under the water.

A few years later the steamer *Connecticut* left the harbour of Portland, Maine on the east coast of the United States. About noon, in full daylight, *Connecticut* was between Nahant and the

Graves when 'the monster was seen approaching.' Some of the male passengers on the pleasure steamer bundled into a small boat to row toward the creature. Despite their good intentions of the men, their oarsmanship did not match their brave intentions and they tangled their oars and got nowhere. The serpent eased toward the boat, passed about an oar's length away and although some of the men bemoaned the lack of a harpoon others were glad that nobody was so foolhardy.

The sea off Maine was busy at that time, with at least three other serpents seen, with lengths from 60 to 150 feet. The passengers of *Connecticut* recommended that a whaling ship should be stationed there to hunt the creatures down.

In August 1850 a serpent was sighted again, this time in Dublin Bay, off Ireland. A man named Hogan had taken a small private party in his yacht for a pleasure cruise. At about half past six in the evening they were between Sutton and Dalkey when they saw what they called a monster rushing toward Howth Point. They were about half a mile from the serpent and thought it had a head like an eel and body that was coiled up like a snake. According to the witnesses, the serpent moved at around twenty miles an hour and left a wake behind it. They thought the serpent was about 100 feet [30 metres] long.

That same month, off Dingle in Ireland, there was another strange sighting. Lord Nelson of the Royal Irish Fisheries Company was sailing through the Blasket Sound when the crew saw what they thought was a fog on the water about quarter of a mile ahead. When they closed with the fog, they realised it was in fact the head and neck of a large serpent. Never having seen anything like this before, the sailors were terrified when the serpent stopped and stared at them for what seemed a long time before it dived into the sea.

It was in September 1871 that Captain McTaggart of the brigantine *Onward*, en-route to Benin from Liverpool sighted a sea serpent. Captain McTaggart reported he was about sixty days out of Liverpool, between Cape Palmas and Grand Bassa, when he became aware that huge shoals of fish surrounded the vessel.

He said that there were sharks, porpoises and many other kinds of fish. Captain McTaggart was an experienced African trader but he had never seen the like before. About eight the next morning as he went forward to take observations of the sun, Captain McTaggart saw something in the water on the starboard bow. Unsure what it was, he called the officers and crew to give their opinion.

'That's a sea serpent!'

All the men on board *Onward* agreed that they had seen nothing like it before. The head was about eight feet out of the water, very broad, and surmounted by what looked like a coronet. As it moved rapidly through the water, the spray on either side looked as if it came from the bows of a ship. After a couple of minutes, the strange creature stopped, and Captain McTaggart examined it closely. About ten feet aft of the head was a large fin that stood two feet proud of the water, with a smaller fin further back. The creature had scales that were 'large and of a beautiful colour.' The head and shoulders of this creature were immensely broad, while the body tapered away some 180 or 200 feet to a tail like a mackerel.

After a few minutes the serpent 'shot ahead again at great speed and was soon lost to view.' Captain McTaggart believed that it was the presence of this creature that had brought the vast shoals of fish the previous day. It might be possible that an undersea eruption had disturbed the animal, whatever it was, from some deep sea trench. Perhaps it was a giant squid, imperfectly observed, with its broad, blunt head and the trailing tentacles? At this space of time, it is unlikely if the truth will ever be known, so Captain McTaggart's sea serpent will probably always be a mystery of the sea.

The very next year, yet another sea monster was sighted, this time much closer to land. Over a hundred people saw what was described as a long and black animal that tumbled about in Belhaven Bay off East Lothian. The creature swam near to the shore and headed west, occasionally stretching its full length so that both the head and tail were out of the water although more often the 'apparent coils of the body' were observed. The serpent was estimated at 'upwards of a hundred feet in length' and up to three feet broad.

This mysterious creature was in sight for fifteen minutes and the *Scotsman* believed that it was either the 'great plesiosaurus' or a 'near relative of the same family. It might also have been a ribbon fish, for such creatures have been cast up on this coast.

Yet, should there be any rational explanation? Perhaps there is always a need for the mysterious and the unexplained. Every age has created its own mysteries, from the dragons of the middle ages to the UFOs that are sometimes supposedly seen above our skies. The sea monsters could merely be another manifestation of a primeval desire for something beyond the known, a response to the solid facts that scientists produce, then alter, then alter again.

Surely experienced, practical master mariners would know exactly what lived in the sea and would recognise what they saw. In which case, there may well be undiscovered creatures inhabiting the dark depths not far beyond our coasts.

Stories of sea monsters abounded when men sailed in small boats, but it is only a comparative few that have survived. In page 22 of his *Memorials of Cellardyke*, published in 1879, George Gourlay mentioned a story that was current in Buchan around 1790, when a 'terrible sea monster' surfaced near a fishing boat and with a 'single toss of' his 'dreadful tail' brushed away their fishing tackle 'with as little effort as the strong winds.' This creature was described as having 'a head as big as a drave boat, covered with bristles, grey in colour, but long and shaggy as the tangles on the skerry.' It was said to be 'the size of the whale' while possessing the 'swiftness and ferocity of the shark.' This was quite a formidable creature then, for the men of an open boat to encounter in the cold seas off north eastern Scotland.

Both the 'Northern Ensign' and the 'East of Fife Record' published the sighting of a sea serpent by an Orcadian sea captain in 1860. Captain Taylor from South Ronaldsay was a 'gentleman of unimpeachable veracity and great intelligence.' His log book for 25th April records that while in 'latitude 12 degrees 7 minutes south and longitude 93 degrees 52 min east' he felt a 'strong sensation as if the ship was trembling.' Captain Taylor climbed the fore rigging and 'saw an enormous serpent shaking the bowsprit with his mouth.' With about thirty feet of the serpent out of the water, its' body 'about the circumference of a very wide crinoline petticoat' stretched right under the ship so that the tail was 'abaft of the stern.' Taylor estimated the serpent to be at least 300 feet long, and described it as having a black back with shaggy main, large glaring eyes and a horn on its forehead. Its jaws alone he estimated as eight feet long. Although the ship *British Banner* was under full sail and travelling at 10 knots, the serpent stopped her completely, detaching the 'bowsprit with the jib-boom sails and rigging.'

After the serpent swallowed the foretopmast staysail, jib and flying jib, it withdrew a little, and then returned to 'scratch himself against the side of the ship, making a most extraordinary noise.' Only when a whale surfaced a mile away did the serpent disappear, swimming toward the newcomer and in the process striking the ship with its tail and 'staving in all the starboard quarter gallery.'

The fact that the serpent moved toward the whale is interesting, for sperm whales and giant squids are said to be deadly enemies. Perhaps the serpent was a squid that had risen from the deep and its length was a distorted view of the tentacles? Or perhaps the experienced Captain would recognise a squid when he saw one and the creature was indeed a serpent.

The sea around the Orkney Islands seemed to be tormented by a colony of strange creatures. There was the Stronsay Beast, and the thing that attacked young Alec Groundwater in the 1850s. A local man, John Peace first found the remains of the Stronsay Beast in September 1808, and was not at all sure what it was. It seemed to be a long, serpent like creature, around 55 feet long that the tide had cast up on the shore. Ever since that time there has been speculation as to what it could have been, with most sceptics settling for a basking shark. If so, it must have been a giant, as the largest basking sharks barely top forty feet.

Alec Groundwater was only a child when he had his encounter with the unknown. He was on the shore at Orphir, staring over Scapa Flow when something rose out of the water. Not surprisingly, Alec did not give a detailed description, but he said the creature had a long mane and a broad flat head with a wide mouth with teeth. It lunged at Alec a number of times before returning into the sea, resurfaced for a last look and disappeared again. Whatever it was, the encounter must have been terrifying to a young boy, but other, more mature observers also saw strange creatures off Orkney.

In 1905 two fishermen reported a creature with a body like a horse, 'covered with a scaly surface and spotted' and in 1919 five fishermen off the headland of Brimsness in Hoy saw a creature with a neck as thick as 'an elephant's foreleg.' In an interview with *The Orcadian* one man recalled that the neck was at least five feet out of the water and estimated that the creature would be between eighteen and twenty feet long.

Eighteen years later, men on Fair Isle thought they saw a large creature approaching them but it did not come close enough to be identified, remaining off shore for most of the day. Later that year of 1937 Mr John Brown, lighthouse keeper at Pentland Skerries and therefore a man with great experience of sea life saw what he described as a 'great object' rising out of the water. This creature, he thought, could have been up to thirty feet tall, 'round shaped and there appeared to be a head on it.'

For all these unknown or unidentified creatures, those that are known are just as deadly. For example there is the swordfish, which in 1817 attacked the whaling ship *Foxhound* in the southern ocean. It was said that the sword thrust entirely through the copper sheathing and the timber and penetrated a foot into the hold. The sword was so firmly stuck that it remained in place until *Foxhound* returned home to England. There is also the Pacific blue tinged octopus that uses its beak to inject venom. So fast acting that antidotes do not work, it can kill a grown man in two hours, but even it pales beside the sea wasp, a jellyfish that infests the Queensland coast. If it stings a human, the victim will break into a quick sweat, lose his sight, choke on his own breath and probably die within a few minutes. It is a creature to be feared, but is probably matched by the Stonefish, that camouflages itself as a stone and has 13 poisonous spines in its back. If a careless foot should stand on one of the spines, the resulting agony could lead to delirium and a painful death. None of the mythical sea monsters are as deadly.

Chapter Twelve
Keepers of the Light

In the autumn of 1995 a story circulated around the Maritime Provinces of Canada. It concerned a radio conversation between a United States ship and Canadian authorities just off the Newfoundland coast. The conversation was something like this:

Americans: 'Please divert your course 15 degrees to the north to avoid a collision.'

Canadians: 'Recommend that you divert your course 15 degrees to the south to avoid a collision.'

Americans: 'This is the captain of a US Navy vessel. I say again, divert your course.'

Canadians: 'No, I say again; you divert your course.'

Americans: 'This is the Aircraft carrier USS *Abraham Lincoln*, the second largest ship in the

United States Atlantic fleet. We are accompanied by three destroyers, three cruisers and numerous support vessels. I demand that you change your course 15 degrees north. That's one five degrees north, or counter measures will be undertaken to ensure the safety of this ship.'

Canadians: 'This is a lighthouse. Your call.'

Today, lighthouses ensure that the coasts of many countries are safe for mariners. They send their beam of safety across some of the wildest water in the world and warn of fog and rocks. Mariners depend on them, but at one time not everybody agreed that lighthouses were a good thing.

At one time the coast of England was plagued with wreckers. The south coast was particularly notorious, so that the locals even had a special prayer: 'Oh God, protect ships at sea from the storm, but if they must run aground, let it be on our shore.'

Just in case the Lord was not paying attention, Wreckers did all they could to help. They might place lights on rocky headlands to make seamen believe that they were the guiding lights of a harbour. They could also attach lanterns to the horns of grazing cattle as a replacement for the lights of a village. If the ship master was unsure of his position, he was more likely to run aground, and there would be little mercy from the coast dwellers.

The South West of England was particularly prone to these wreckers, and for that reason the local landlords were said to object to lighthouses being built on their land, as they would lose valuable revenue. There was a Right of Wreck along parts of the English coast. That meant that the coast dwellers had the right to possess the remains of a ship and its cargo, provided always that there were no survivors. On many occasions seamen lived through the horrors of shipwreck and struggled ashore, torn and battered by rocks, only to face the knives of the Wreckers. History has put a gloss of glamour on these proceedings, but there was only sordid murder in the surf for the seamen.

But there were wreckers in other parts of the world as well. In the 1880s the people along the coast of Newfoundland and Labrador were notorious as wreckers. One case that brought the true facts to the world's attention was that of the Glasgow vessel *Eirene*, bound from Montreal to Glasgow in September 1879. She carried a full cargo of cattle, flour and grain but was wrecked in Red Bay, Labrador. The ship master checked the cargo, saw it was safe, checked the ship and saw she was not badly damaged and was very hopeful of getting her off safe and sound. However, he was overly optimistic. Although the local Collector of Customs was quickly on the scene to offer his protection, a horde of men swarmed aboard to plunder everything they could. To the fishermen of Conception Bay, it was a way of life.

The master of *Eirene* hurried to the nearest telegraph station and cabled the revenue service in St John's Newfoundland to ask for help. They replied in the negative, saying it was not their job, and if any help came, the ship master paid for the expense.

The Attorney general at St John's moved swiftly against the wreckers, but a jury found them all not guilty. When the officials arrived at the wreck they found the plunderers hard at work but rather than arrest them, they merely forced them to give up two thirds of their plunder and let them go free with the remaining third.

Throughout the centuries, every storm threw up wrecks around the coasts of Britain, with the stronger storms wreaking terrible devastation among coastal shipping. The shores and beaches of the four nations of Britain were littered with vessels and pieces of wreckage, as well as the corpses of drowned sailors. Most of these bodies were treated with respect and given a Christian burial, but in some places they were not so well cared for. Near St Ann's Head in Pembrokeshire, the people who lived by the coast tended to strip the copses of anybody cast ashore. For example in the storm of December 1868 a French vessel with fifty of a crew was lost, with thirteen cast ashore between St Ann and Dale, and all were stripped stark. Female passengers were treated with the same lack of concern as male, much to the horror of the respectable.

Not only the poor profited from perished ships. In 1643, Father Gilbert Blackhal was bound for Scotland when a storm blew him into the sheltered harbour of Lindisfarne. He told of an undignified squabble over a cask full of beaver hats that formed part of the cargo of a wrecked ship. Two of the most avaricious men present were a local gentleman and William Mitton, the parish priest. Past the verbal stage, both men drew weapons and 'the minister did sore wound the gentleman.' Such treasures as the sea provided had helped the island sustain its economy since mediaeval times. Today Lindisfarne prefers to remove money from the tourist by more legal methods.

Naturally it was the landowners who profited most by these wrecks. Equally naturally they did not want to lose such a lucrative source of easy profit. However, successive governments and harbour authorities attempted to make the seas a safer place. In 1566 an Act made it illegal to remove 'sea-marks' or those features on the coast that seafarers used to clarify their position. If anybody moved or damaged such a mark, he could be fined £100, or banished as an outlaw.

Mediaeval monks did their best to make the seas safer. For instance the Abbot of Arbroath put a bell on the Inchcape Rock, eleven miles off the Angus Coast, only for a pirate and wrecker to remove the warning. According to legend, the Wrecker himself became a victim to the terrible rock, which was barely exposed at low tide and completely hidden when the sea was high. There was also Great Mew Stone island, a few cables' lengths off Wembury Point in south Devon, where mediaeval monks placed an oil lamp on top of a tower to warn passing sailors. Lossiemouth in Moray had a holy man who stalked the skerries with a lantern to warn passing ships: Halliman Skerries is named in his honour. Perhaps slightly later was the stone tower that was built on the Farne Islands, off Northumberland, on top of which a fire was lit in times of bad weather. These were the islands on which the famous Grace Darling lived, when she and her father made heroic efforts to save the crew of *Forfarshire*.

Not too far away, off Whitley Bay in Northumberland is Bait Island, also known as St Mary's. This tiny islet was once home to a cemetery that held the last remains of drowned seamen, with a light in the mediaeval chapel to act as warning to passing ships. When the lighthouse was erected, the inhabitants of the graveyard were removed to the mainland.

Some reefs became known for the ships that they wrecked. For instance the Godrevy Islands in St Ives Bay in North Cornwall were known for the reef that hid to the north west. Local fishermen called this reef 'Plenty-to-come-yet because it was home to hundreds of lobsters. However, at least two ships perished here. In 1640 a vessel ran aground here, and is recalled more for the loss of King Charles' clothes than for the sixty human lives that ended. However it was the loss of the steamer *Nile* in 1854 that reminded the authorities of the hidden danger. A lighthouse was built, allegedly the one Virginia Woolfe used in her novel *To the Lighthouse.*

In the 17th century Lowestoft, Caister and Dungeness possessed warning beacons, while in 1687 Dundee planted coal lights to mark the safest route through the sandbanks that bedevilled the approached to the Tay. The unfortunate first keeper of the early lighthouse on the Island of May drowned in the Forth, and a local witch accepted the credit for their demise. She was burned.

A later keeper, together with his wife and five of his six children were asphyxiated with the fumes from the coal fire. Life could be tough in the safety trade.

By the late 18th century the seas had become busier and people were concerned about the number of ships that were being wrecked. In 1800 Britain was losing around one vessel a day, and in times of storm the number was terrifyingly high, with consequent loss of life and money. The authorities built more lighthouses, and dedicated men spent much of their working lives surrounded by some of the most savage seas in the world. Working in small teams, these men worked a four hour shift in the light room, unable to leave the light, forbidden to read a word in that time, or listen to the radio. He was alone save for the slowly circulating light and the immense span of sea whose waves could be grasping up at the slender building, hour after terrifying hour.

Many of the lighthouses around Britain have tales and legends attached to them. For instance the lighthouse men at Sule Skerry, alone with three thousand miles of Atlantic rollers, were said to hear an ethereal choir singing from the horizon. It was said that these men listened for the sound, hating to miss even a single note. Sule Skerry, of course, thirty miles west of Orkney, was a place of mystery long before the pencil-slim lighthouse first rose to challenge the ocean, for this was the supposed abode of the legendary king seal that could turn into a human on Midsummer Eve.

There was also the famous Flannan Island group, where all three men vanished at the dawn of the 20th century. These islands are 18 miles west of Lewis, with the largest, Eilean Mor (that simply means Big Island in Gaelic) being only 39 acres but rising to nearly 100 metres. In December 1899 the Northern Lighthouse Board built a 74 foot high lighthouse to guide ships around Cape Wrath (the Cape of Turning) and sent a three man crew to look after it. Life on the Flannan Islands was not easy. The keepers had to raise poultry and sheep to eat; one keeper died falling from the light and four men drowned when their boat overturned on the choppy approach. However the light was necessary to guide ships through vicious seas.

Nearly a year later the steamer *Archtor* passed the lighthouse and reported that there was no light showing. His report did not reach the Northern Lighthouse Board and as the weather was stormy, it was not until the 26th December that the relief lighthouse keepers arrived at the Flannan Islands. There were three keepers on the light: Thomas Marshall, Donald McArthur and James Ducat. The relief keepers knew at once that things were not right: there was no flag flying to indicate that it was time for the relief, and there was no keeper waiting at the landing place.

Captain Jim Harvie of the relief ship fired a signal flare, which shot up, shone briefly and died without response. Nor was there any reply when Harvie sounded the ship's whistle. The Relief Keeper, Joseph Moore, stepped into the dingy and rowed to the lighthouse to see what had happened. He found the gate to the lighthouse grounds and the door to the keeper's quarters was closed but the kitchen door inside was open. The clock on the wall had stopped for want of winding and there was no fire laid in the grate, despite the bitter cold season of the year.

Worst of all; there were no keepers present. All three men had vanished.

Four men came to thoroughly examine the lighthouse and its surroundings. They found the lamps cleaned and refilled and two out of three sets of foul weather gear missing from the clothes store. At some time heavy weather had damaged the West landing, twisting the heavy iron railings and shifting a ton-weight stone high up the steep slopes of the island. Ducat was a man of 20 years' experience in lighthouses, yet he had specifically asked not to be sent to the Flannan Islands. His log was written in full up to the 13th December and there were notes for the 14th and 15th, so it seems that was the day when the men vanished. Researchers consider that the accident, whatever it was, occurred in the late morning of the 15th.

A number of experienced lighthouse keepers inspected the light and decided that a series of huge waves had approached the island when two of the men were on the landing stage. When the third keeper, McArthur had seen the waves coming he had run to warn the others but all three had been washed away. Others disputed this theory, saying that although there had been wild weather, it had calmed by the fifteenth and anyway, the keepers would not have ventured outside if the weather was bad. There were darker theories propounded, such as an attack by aliens, a giant bird or that one of the keepers lost his reason and attacked the other two. The strangest theory of all claimed that the local spirits on these mysterious islands killed the three keepers out of spite. That harkens back to the old history of the Flannan Islands, as they were always thought of as islands of mystery and loneliness, where Hebrideans performed age-old rituals after they landed.

Other Scottish lighthouses were nearly as wild. At the Rhinns of Islay, at the southern tip of the Inner Hebrides, the keepers could look out to a sea where seven tides met in the infamous Overseas Race that hazarded even powerful vessels. Of course there were always natural hazards for the lighthouse men. For example, the 'East of Fife Record' for July 26 1872 carried a story of a 'violent thunderstorm' over Berwick that caused a lightning strike on the Berwick lighthouse. According to the account, 'the electric fluid struck a ventilator on the roof and entered the building, passed across the stone floor in the upper storey, and down the staircase, leaving traces of its course through all the three storeys of the building down to the basement. In the bottom floor part of the wooden flooring was torn up but no one was injured.'

However, perhaps the most shocking story comes from the Small's Rock off Pembrokeshire, where keepers first learned the folly or working in pairs. Two keepers had just begun their three-month tour of duty when one became ill. Sickness was an accepted part of Victorian life, and without medical help it was perhaps no surprise when the keeper wasted away and eventually died. The surviving keeper, knowing that he had now to supervise the light single-handed, prepared his friend for burial.

First he wrapped him in a canvas sail, sewing him in to ensure he was secure, and then he said a short prayer and dragged the body toward the sea. The keeper hesitated for a moment, contemplating the loneliness he would have to endure over the next three months, but sighed and prepared to drop his friend into the sea. It was only then that he realised his position. There were no witnesses out here, and nobody's word save his own that his friend had died of disease. It was not unknown for lighthouse keepers to quarrel; it was natural for two men, trapped in isolation for months to resent the other's irritating habits. Arguments could escalate into violence, even into murder. He might be accused of murdering his colleague.

The keeper nodded. No; he could not bury his companion yet. First he had to tell somebody what had happened, show them that there were no wounds on the body. Accordingly, he tried to signal to every ship that passed, but in the days before radio, when ships tried to give lighthouses and their dangerous rocks a wide berth, nobody replied. The keeper began to resent his dead friend, and dragged him outside the lighthouse. To keep the body safe, he hung it, still secure in its canvas shroud, on the galley that surrounded the light.

Without the body, there was more space inside the lighthouse, but every time he looked outside, the keeper saw the shrouded shape of his comrade swaying against the glass. At night, the light slowly turned, so one minute there was darkness and memory, the next there was the body, ghostly white in the sudden gleam. The keeper began to imagine things, each sound of the wind was transformed into his friend clawing clear of the canvas; each squall of a gull was his comrade complaining against the chill of the night.

Days passed; then weeks, sliding into long, slow months and finally the relief boat set out with a new crew. The keeper waited for them, frothing at the mouth with madness after spending months alone with his fears and the decomposing mess that had been his companion.

The story says that after this incident, British lighthouses carried a three man crew. Now, of course, the lights are automatic and there is no reason for men to spend long lonely months surrounded by the sea, watching and waiting.

However, lighthouses in other lands could have dangers unknown in Britain. On the 24th July 1836 hostile Indians attacked Key Biscano Lighthouse in Florida and burned it to the ground. The Lords Commissioners of the Admiralty sent out a circular to the Customs and Excise offices in Britain, asking them to warn any seafarers who passed that way. It cannot be often that Indians and seamen met, but the sea coast was a strange place.

Chapter Thirteen
Eating the Ship's Boy

One of the great taboos of history is cannibalism, humans eating humans, either for ritual reasons, religious reasons or simply for food. Cannibalism has been shunned, relegated to horror stories or traveller's tales from the darkest areas of the world. It was presumed that cannibalism was confined to the distant past, or to uncivilised foreigners. However, that was a comfortable misconception; cannibalism was alive and well and sat as a forbidden shadow on the fringes of the mind of many seamen.

The odd rumour and suspicion about cannibalism at sea emerged from time to time, but in September 1884 a case of definite and deliberate cannibalism came to the court at Falmouth in south west England. The vessel had been a yacht named *Mignonette* and the master, mate and some of the crew had killed and eaten a 17 year old boy named Michael Parker on the high seas on 20 July that year. The master was Captain Thomas Dudley, a Surrey man and a greengrocer, although he had been a seaman for many years before he turned to retail. He was a very experienced yachtsman. His wife was the headmistress of the girl's department of Newtown Board School. Dudley had not at first wished to take command of Mignonette, but when he was offered £100 down payment, and another £100 on arrival he agreed.

Mignonette was elderly but a good sea boat; she was a 33 ton yacht. Jack Want, A Sydney lawyer, had bought her purely to be able to boast that he owned an English built yacht. *Mignonette* left on her voyage from Fay's Yard in Southampton on 19 May. The weather was excellent at first; they called at Madeira for provisions, and then sailed on, southward to their destiny. There were no problems until the 5 July when the weather grew stormy. They were in 27.10 south, 9.50 west, about 1600 miles from the Cape of Good Hope. Captain Thomas Dudley ordered *Mignonette* to heave to until the weather abated. About four in the evening he called the watch and brought in the square sail, then ordered the covers put on the after hatch. No sooner was that done than Edwin Stephens, the mate who was at the wheel shouted: 'Look out!'

Dudley glanced underneath the boom and saw a massive wave rising above them. He wrapped both arms around the boom as the wave broke over them. When the water passed, Dudley looked around.

'My God,' said Edmund Brooks, who emerged from down below, 'her side is knocked in.'

Dudley stared; the lee bulwarks were completely gone, washed away by the heavy sea, and worse, the entire lee side of the vessel was stove in so she was open to every wave that came. Dudley had no choice but to launch the fourteen foot long dinghy and abandon Mignonette. He sent the ship's boy, Parker, to fetch a beaker of fresh water for the lifeboat. Parker grabbed the beaker and threw it overboard, intending to collect it later. Dudley lifted the binnacle and lowered it into the boat as well. The mate and the seaman named

Brooks joined Parker in the boat while Dudley slipped into the cabin to pick up his sextant and whatever food he could find.

The cabin was waist deep in surging seawater, so Dudley had little time; he took hold of the sextant and the chronometer, snatched half a dozen tins that he hoped contained food. By that time the men in the boat were shouting out to him that the ship was sinking and he had better hurry or he would be drowned. Dudley scurried back on deck and dropped into the boat, with his tins rattling onto the bottom boards. He took hold of the oars and backed water, just as Mignonette slipped beneath the surface of the water. It had been less than five minutes since the wave struck her beam on.

They rowed around the disturbed water where *Mignonette* had gone down, picking up a tin of turnips, the chronometer and the sextant. They did not find the beaker of fresh water. Dudley made a sea anchor from the bottom boards and binnacle so the boat rode easier, but they were still making water. They realised that there was a leak in the boat, found a plank that had been damaged when they dropped it in the sea and plugged the hole. They had a bailer in the boat, but only two one-and-a-half pound tins of turnips between them, and not a drop of water. Night was coming on, and the sea was getting higher.

A great moon rose as the darkness crept in, and a shark nosed around the boat. It pushed against the planking but swam away again. The night crept on; day dawned and they steered for the Cape, more in hope than expectation. The next day passed; and the next; and the next. On the fourth day a turtle swam close; they hauled it into the boat, killed it and it supplied them with food and liquid. They finished the second tin of turnips that day and drank some of the blood of the turtle. The rest they poured into the wooden box that had held the chronometer, but salt water had got in and left it undrinkable.

The days passed; six, seven, eight days, with the trade wind still blowing hard from the South East. They used their oilskin coats to catch rain from the squalls, cursed when salt water contaminated most of their hard won reservoir. They finished the turtle on the thirteenth day, chewing the skin in the vain hope it could produce saliva. On the fifteenth day, starving, black-tongued with thirst, desperate, they attached their shirts to an upright oar to make a mast and sail, but by then there was little hope. They had eaten nothing and drunk nothing for days. Only then did they come to a terrible choice.

Captain Dudley decided that they could not all survive with the limited supplies they had, but if one of them was killed, the others could eat him to survive. He proposed that they cast lots, but Stevens and Brooks did not agree to that. Brooks turned the idea down flat: 'let's all die together' he said. Dudley then asked the men if they were married and if they had a family. Stevens had a family of five, while Dudley had three children of his own. They looked at Richard Parker, the young ship's boy. He lay on the bottom of the boat, raving and half mad. He had drunk salt sea water; he was in miserable agony. Dudley, Stevens and Brooks made a pact between them. Unless they saw a sail or land by dawn, or unless it rained, they would kill young Parker. By eight the next morning it was full daylight; nothing broke the hard line of the horizon, neither land nor ship. Dudley, Brook and the mate signalled to each other that somebody should kill the ship's boy. Brooks refused; he was 39 years old and had been at sea for 30 years. Perhaps he remembered his early years as a ship's boy. Rather than murder the child he withdrew to the bow and covered his face with his hands. The mate was as humane.

'I will try and do it' Dudley said.

He asked Stephens to hold Parker's legs if he struggled or tried to escape. Dudley gave a prayer to ask forgiveness for what he was about to do and asked that their souls would be saved. 'Now Dick,' Dudley said quietly, 'your time has come.'

Lying in the bottom of the boat, starved, half crazed with thirst and far from home, Parker removed the hand that had been covering his face and looked up: 'What, me sir?' he asked.

'Yes, my boy,' Dudley said, placed his knife at the side of the boy's neck and sliced open the jugular.

Parker was dead within ten seconds and Dudley caught the blood that flowed from his neck. The three survivors drank what they could from the bailer. 'I sucked it down' Brooks later admitted. After that Dudley used the same knife to cut Parker's clothes off him so the boy lay stark and white. Then they cut out the boy's liver and heart and ate them raw, with the dark blood dribbling into their shaggy beards. With some strength restored they washed and covered Parker's dead body. The three men lived off Parker for the next four days, and when the body began to rot, they sliced off the bad parts, washed the remainder in salt water and ate it. Parker kept them alive.

Twenty four days after the wreck, Brooks gave a shout. He was steering but suddenly looked up 'A sail!' he said and the three survivors began to pray earnestly for rescue. Dudley ordered that the sail should be brought in; they took the oars and tried to row to windward to come as close as possible to the passage of the unknown vessel.

It took an hour of desperate work to get within hailing distance of the vessel, which proved to be the German barque *Montezuma*. Her master, Captain Simmeson, heaved to and helped the three men on board. After 24 days in a small boat they were so weak they could not stand, burned by exposure, bearded, emaciated and unwashed.

The lifeboat was picked up at 24.28 south and 27.22 west. The survivors had travelled 1,050 miles from the spot *Mignonette* had sunk.

Even as the German crew rescued the survivors, they noticed the pieces of human flesh that were all that remained on the ship's boy. Dudley and the others did not hide what had happened, and when the Germans wished to bury what was left of Parker at sea, Dudley asked that the remains be retained.

It took *Montezuma* 28 days to reach port, and during the voyage Captain Simmeson and his crew could not have been kinder to the cannibals.

Before his trial at Falmouth, Captain Dudley wrote a letter to his wife, in which he stated: 'No harm can come to me or any of us my dear; you are sure and trust in God to give you strength to bear the horrid lies that are in the papers.'

Convicted of murder, Dudley and the mate were not hanged as their sentence was commuted to six months in prison.

Was that a strange tale? Here is an even stranger twist: half a century before the disaster to Mignonette, the American author Edgar Allan Poe wrote a short story 'The Narrative of Arthur Gordon Pym' in which a ship's boy named Richard Parker was killed and eaten by his shipmates. Now that is indeed strange.

Chapter Fourteen
The Curse of Women

There are many theories why it was once thought unlucky to have a woman on board a ship. Some are purely practical, for the presence of a woman may invoke jealousy on a long voyage, and that could create trouble. Others are more ethereal, such as the belief that the ship was a female and would resent any competition. Such beliefs lasted until recently. Even on land, the wives of seamen had to be careful. For instance, the wife of a Scottish fisherman could never wash on the day her man went to sea, in case she blew up a storm that would wash him away, while if a Caithness wife blew on her oatcakes to cool them, to place a loaf upside down was also dangerous, for bread in that position resembled a capsized boat. Fisherwomen were also banned from whistling, for that sounded like a gale through the rigging, and there were even cases when a fisherman drew blood from his wife to bring him luck at the fishing.

However, fisherwomen seemed to have very strong marriage bonds, with women every bit as important as their men. Indeed, a Scottish fisherman was not reckoned a full man until he was married. Other seamen also liked the company of women, hence the old saying that a sailor had a wife in every port. In view of this attraction that women had for seamen on land, banning them from ships seems remarkably mysterious. It is even more mysterious when it is realised how many women actually did work at sea, often as an accepted part of the ship's company and accepted, if not welcomed, by the men on board. It was said that the bosun's cry to 'show a leg' in the morning was to identify the women. If a female leg appeared from the hammock, folklore claims that she was permitted to remain a little longer.

The Royal Navy of the 18th and 19th centuries was a powerful force that defeated every enemy that it encountered. The navy defeated the French, Spanish, Dutch, Danes and, eventually, Americans in a series of battles and skirmishes that could be counted as glorious or sordid, depending on one's point of view. In every action, British seamen manned the guns, while powder monkeys ran from the magazine to the cannon, carrying cartridges filled with gunpowder. In theory, these powder monkeys were young boys who were training to become seamen. In practice, many of them were women.

When a seaman named John Nicol wrote his memoirs, he mentioned serving on board *Goliath* where women and boys carrying powder at the battle of the Nile, with 'the women behaved as well as the men.' He also mentioned that some women were wounded and killed in the action, while another gave birth during the battle. There was nothing unusual about women giving birth on board ship; one boy born at the battle of the Glorious First of June was named Daniel Tremendous Mackenzie, his middle name being that of the ship his mother was in. Tristan Jones, amputee yachtsman and author, was born at sea off Tristan da Cunha, while Mrs Anna Nielson gave birth to all her four girls on board ship. In 1892 Laura Atlanti was born in the North Atlantic. In 1893 Daisy Thevan arrived off one of the Caroline Islands in the Pacific. A year or two later, India Kristina Daisy arrived while her mother was sailing in the Indian Ocean, while in 1897 Maori Zelani was born in New Zealand. It seems that some seamen actually welcomed the presence of a pregnant woman on board, as pregnancy meant a new life, although menstruating women were often regarded with something approaching horror.

Another woman known to have given birth on board ship was Mary Buek from Fife, who accompanied her husband to sea when the Navy pressed him. She remained at his side for years, with Mary becoming a mother to Margaret during the cannonade of Copenhagen and becoming a veteran of the battle of Trafalgar. After the battle she prepared Nelson's body for embalming.

Occasionally, the sea mother was single, perhaps because her man had died of disease or fallen victim to any of the innumerable shipboard accidents that killed many more men than battle ever did. Women in labour were invariably confined between two cannon, and if the father was not around, or was not known, the resulting child was a 'son of the gun.'

Most women on board warships at sea were the wives of warrant officers, and the evidence suggests that they played an important part on board. Again it is Nicol who gives some details: 'I was much indebted to the gunner's wife, who gave her husband and me a drink of wine every now and then, which lessened our fatigue much.'

There were twenty known women who served on board Nelson's warships in the guise of men. One at least, William Brown, became captain of the foretop, but these were the exceptions. Most women saw no need to disguise their gender to be useful, for they seemed to have acted as mothers for the youngsters on board and, if Mary Buek is a fair example, unofficial nurses for the sick. The wives of Petty Officers also acted as nurses after the Battle of Navarino in 1827. HMS *Genoa* had nine wives on board, and all played their part.

At the beginning of the eighteenth century there had been hospital ships where women officially worked, but they had such a shocking reputation for drunkenness that the Royal Navy abandoned the idea, preferring male nurses. It seems that, despite this official denial, women continued to act as nurses on ships.

When the ships were in port, of course, they became a temporary home to scores, if not hundreds of women. As soon as a warship arrived in any of the major British naval bases, boatloads of prostitutes rowed out, until every man had a temporary wife. There were some evangelical officers who insisted that each woman must show proof that she was married to her man, but most sensible captains turned a Nelsonian blind eye. As every man had only fourteen inches breadth of hammock space, the sights and sounds below decks can scarcely be conceived. In a major warship there could be five hundred men and four hundred women crammed in together, living, drinking, eating, quarrelling, loving and singing.

Although most of these women would be wives of convenience, there was a recognised procedure for simple marriages between seamen and shoe based women. Until 1753 seamen and their women could step over a sword while intoning the formula:

'Leap rogue and jump whore
and then you are married for evermore'

These were no clergy present at such a marriage, but they were seen as legal at a time when life was often short and a seaman's time on shore very limited. If, as often happened, the husband disappeared, the wife could claim his wages. There were other arrangements, whereby a seaman would come ashore after a voyage and splice himself to a woman until his next trip. For the duration of their time together, the couple acted as a faithful man and wife. Seamen in the 19th century looked after the womenfolk of the crew in a different fashion. Most ships had what were termed 'widow's men', which were imaginary seamen. These men drew pay, which was given to the widows of men that had once belonged to the ship.

Merchant vessels could also carry women. Many ship's masters took their wives to sea, and on occasion the wife made decisions if her husband was ill. In American whaling vessels, these women were named as 'assistant navigators' but British wives had no need for deception. Perhaps that was because the owners knew that these wives could be formidable, ensuring a strict parsimony with the vessel's supplies, but they could also darn socks or comfort the younger first voyagers. Until very recently, however, there were very few women in charge of British ships. There are a few shaded references to Hebridean women, the daughters of island chiefs, who commanded galleys in the mediaeval period, and one known Scottish woman, Betsy Miller from Saltcoats, who both owned and captained a Clyde based collier. There was also Katherine Fleming from Saint Andrews, who received a permit as skipper of the St Andrews University fishing boat *Aphrodite* in 1939. *Aphrodite* was a 20-foot yawl that fished in St Andrew Bay for scientific purposes, and Katherine Fleming commanded her for a number of years, even after she was married.

And, of course, there were women who travelled as passengers. Occasionally, women passengers were more trouble than any amount of men. It was on *Lady Shore*, a vessel transporting female convicts to Australia in 1797, that the only successful convict transport mutiny occurred. Unfortunately, it was the guards who mutinied, and the convicts became servants to Spanish ladies rather than convicts in New South Wales. Nearly seventy years later, in 1864, *Dunbar Castle*, commanded by Captain David Carvosso was carrying 10 married couples and ninety single women emigrants to Sydney. One evening in the South Atlantic, near the end of the second dog watch, a riot erupted from the single woman's quarters and the matron fled to the deck, sobbing hysterically. A few minutes later the ship's doctor followed, minus his trousers and with his shirt hanging in shreds.

It seems possible that the women objected to the doctor's attempts to medically examine them, and retaliated by attempting to examine him. As the trouble continued, Captain Carvosso descended to the women's quarters. The female's ringleader, a large woman from the North of England, was stripped to waist, waiting for him with her fists raised.

'What the devil next?' cried Captain Carvosso, but rather than fight the mutineer, he blasted her with the same lung power that could reach the fore topgallant mast in a Cape Horn Snorter. However, he did threaten to turn the hose on to the women unless they obeyed orders. Impressed, the women returned to their bunks, and peace returned to *Dunbar Castle.*

Women passengers could also be excellent smugglers. It was very well known that many of the women who swarmed aboard the Royal Naval ships had rum concealed about their persons, while in 1806 the fisherwomen of Arbroath were warned about their smuggling habits. Scotswomen seemed to be frequently involved in smuggling, for there was also the case of Maggie McConnel, of Dailly Bay in the South West of Scotland. When a cargo was run in from the Isle of Man, she knocked down the local exciseman and threw her skirt over his head to keep him quiet and blind while the menfolk removed the goods. It was an unfair contest, for Maggie was known to lift cattle in her day job on the farm. Sometimes women seemed to go to a great deal of trouble to smuggle what seems an everyday item. For instance in August 1821 an Irish woman was caught smuggling window glass. She had three pieces, each thirteen inches long and ten broad suspended beneath her broad skirts. One piece hung beside each thigh, and one behind her. Presumable she did not sit down for the duration of the voyage.

However, there were occasions when women passengers showed their mettle. According to the 'East of Fife Record', in 1868 the British ship *Macduff* was sailing in Eastern waters when a strange sail showed over the horizon. Even that late in the nineteenth century the seas were not entirely safe from pirates. Although the golden age of European pirates such as Teach, Roberts and Avery was long gone, there were Chinese junks, Arab dhows, seadyaks, Malays and sundry other people that it was best to avoid. When the three masted schooner drew close, the master of *Macduff* cast a wary eye on her. Sure enough, she was packed with ugly looking men, at least one hundred, possibly as many as one hundred and fifty; far too many for a merchant ship, and too well armed to be pilgrims.

It was lucky that *Macduff* had some soldiers on board, but the master was worried about the women. Would they panic? Most Victorian men believed that women were weak creatures, liable to swoon at any emergency. The master watched them as the pirates closed, but rather than faint, the women took their positions beside the men. There was gunfire across the sea as the soldiers aimed and fired while the women loaded and gave encouragement. After half an hour the pirate ship withdrew, and *Macduff* sailed on to Melbourne, proud of her fighting females.

Other sea women fought as professionals. The pirate women Anne Bonny and Mary Read are well known, but there were many others. During the reign of Elizabeth of England, Sir John Killigrew was the Vice-Admiral of Cornwall and one of the Commissioners for Piracy, but his mother was a bit of a rogue. She had the habit of taking her boat into Falmouth harbour to pirate any vessel that took her fancy. On one occasion she took a boatload of Cornishmen to attack a German ship, murdered some of the crew and looted the vessel. Her daughter in law was just as bad, for when a Spanish merchantman was driven into harbour by bad weather, she commanded a boatload of pirates that robbed and killed the crew.

As well as troublemakers and trouble-shooters, women at sea could prove an embarrassment. In

1867 the East Indiamen *St Lawrence* and *Winch-ester* were sailing from Calcutta to Britain. Each carried half of the 98th Foot, which had been based in India for some years. The captain of every East Indiaman was proud of his ship, knowing that its speed, efficiency and appearance were superior to every other vessel in the fleet, so the voyage became a race. As they approached St Helena, *St Lawrence* saw a sail ahead, and the lookout called out that it was *Winchester.*

'Make all sail!' cried the captain, and watched as *St Lawrence* steadily crept up to *Winchester.* As *St Lawrence* passed her rival, the master unhooked his speaking trumpet and jeered, 'how do you like the look of our stern?' but the Captain of *Winch-ester*'s reply soon deflated his ego.

'Much like a laundry!' he jeered.

With the female passengers berthed aft, they had hung out their washing around the stern gallery, so that *Saint Lawrence* was decorated with a profusion of feminine underclothing, which did nothing for the dignity of her master. For some time after, *Saint Lawrence* was known as the laundry ship.

Other passengers were less official, but probably just as welcome to soldiers posted to foreign stations. In most records of stowaways, it is a young boy who hides on board a ship, usually in the hope of a life of adventure at sea. However on the 20th January 1868 the 'Indian Daily News' reported that the troopship *Flying Foam* had two female stowaways on board. One girl was sixteen; the other seventeen and some of the soldiers had hidden them on board. The crew discovered and cared for the stowaways, but both ran as soon as *Flying Foam* docked. Later on both were discovered living in the veranda of the barracks, and it was assumed that even before they left Britain they had married soldiers without any permission.

Even on shore, women could affect men at sea. Probably the most maritime of any women were the fisher wives. In old Scotland they would help launch the boat, often carry their men to and from the boat, dig up bait, bait the lines and sell the catch as well as knit the seagoing pullovers of their men. In common with their men, they had to be very careful with their behaviour at all times. Whistling was banned, in case it called up a storm, combing her hair after sunset could bring very bad luck to her husband, but if she dreamed of a white sea there was good luck in the offing.

Today, of course, the situation has changed. There are more women serving in the Royal Navy than ever before, and women also work in the merchant navy. Yachtswomen such as Ellen MacArthur and Emma Richardson have proved their capability to sail alongside the best men in the world, with Richardson being the first woman and, at 28, the youngest person, to complete the 29,000- mile Round the World race. The legacy of Grace Darling also lives on, for in the 1990s the Broughty Ferry lifeboat recruited its first female member. Unlike some earlier women, she has no need to hide her femininity, being the mother of two children, but she has worked with the sea since she was ten years of age.

Women have always played a large part in life at sea. They worked as seamen, even taking command. They acted as powder monkeys and nurses. They cohabited with the seamen or travelled as passengers. It seems mysterious then, that they were ever thought unlucky. There are three possible answers. There is the safety aspect, for men liked to be seen as protectors and would not wish for women to be exposed to the dangers at sea. Then there is the sexual worry when the crew of a mixed sex ship might be subject to all sorts of temptation on a long voyage, with jealous rivalries creating trouble. However, the third possibility seems more likely.

In the very early days of sea travel, sailors were respectful of the sea god. Neptune, Poseidon, Mannanan; all were gods of the sea, and all were male. Because seamen hoped not to anger their god, they made their ships female. Seagoing vessels were almost always given feminine names and referred to as 'she' to invoke the natural chivalry of the male sea god. However, the feelings of the ship also had to be considered. She would not take kindly to a rival for her affections, so might turn her spite on any crew who brought a woman on board. Women were seen as unlucky on a seagoing vessel. However, it was sometimes the case that married seamen who sailed with a certain line were also unlucky.

In the 1860s, many British newspapers carried the tale of the Cunard Widows. It seems that two seamen, both of whom sailed with the Cunard Line, married. The seamen waved goodbye to their wives at the quay, promising to see them as soon as the ship returned, and the wives watched from the shore as their husband's ship slipped beneath the horizon.

Life at sea was always unpredictable, with danger from storms, accidents and disease, but it was unfortunate that both the new husbands should fall from the mast on that same voyage. Both were killed, and there were two more grieving widows standing on the quayside. Life was hard for a woman in Victorian Britain and harder still for a widow, so it was not long before both women married again. Being creatures of the sea, they again became attached to seafaring men, and again waved goodbye to their husbands as they sailed on a Cunard ship.

The outward voyage was smooth, with the ship arriving safely in New York. However, accidents can happen even in port, and one man was working on the foreyard when he slipped and fell. A sail broke his fall, and as he lay in hospital he mentioned the fate of his predecessor. The ship sailed the next day, and only one day out the second husband fell from the mainyard and died. Even as his widow again donned her mourning black, the first seaman also died and both women were again widows.

It was pure coincidence of course, but perhaps a topic for seamen to speak of in the short time off watch; just another strange tale of the sea.

Chapter Fifteen
Religion at Sea

The sea and religion has always been intimately linked in both positive and negative fashions. Perhaps it was because of the constant awareness of danger and the often long voyages, or the closeness to nature in all its forms, but seamen could be deeply religious or shockingly blasphemous.

Sometimes the same men could be both, depending on circumstances. As Sir Walter Runciman said, if the men were cursing there was no fear of the ship being sunk; if they were praying, then the ship is in danger. It was a commonly held belief in some Scandinavian ships that swearing was accepted, but blasphemy was highly dangerous, for God or the sea gods could take it personally and might decide to sink the ship. It was blasphemy that condemned the Flying Dutchman to his eternal hell in sailing around the Cape of Storms. The Danes, however, were less tolerant of swearing, which many old time seamen believed to call up a storm.

While Scottish fishermen were very wary of meeting Church ministers while on their way to sea, other mariners of the 18th and 19th century used holy instruments every day. The deck was scrubbed with a lump of stone known as a 'holy-stone', with tradition claiming that the name is ancient, originating from the original place where these useful articles were first found.

The first holystones were said to have come from a ruined church in the south of England. A party of seamen were digging up sand to scrub the deck, and one man, more enterprising or lazier than the rest, took a stone from a nearby church wall as well. When the ship's officers realised that the stone was perfect for scrubbing purposes, the news spread and soon holy stones were common. Using stones from such a place, of course, was also sacrilege, but the seamen sweated out their penance.

Fishermen can be among the most religious of seamen. Even the most casual visit to any British fishing village, or one-time fishing village, will find a number of churches, often from a variety of different denominations. In the 19th century, when Darwin's theory of evolution caused a great furore among the religious establishment, there were a number of religious revivalist movements in Britain and one year fishermen would be known for their roughness, the next they would be heard singing psalms at sea. It was common practise for the beginning of the salmon fishing season to be blessed by the local priest, as in Berwick on Tweed.

In France, Brittany is perhaps the most maritime province. There also priests bless the boats and lead a procession that actually wades through the shallows to the fishing boats as the priests also bless the nets.

The relationship between religion and the sea is ancient. At one time Aidan of Lindisfarne was asked for his blessing when his friend Utta was travelling down to Kent to escort the Queen of Northumbria back home. Aidan handed over a flask of holy oil and made a prophesy. 'You will meet storms and adverse winds. Pour the oil on the sea and the winds will drop and the sea calm.'

The seamen set out, but a storm blew up and they forgot the prophesy until it was almost too late, but the second they poured the oil on the weaves, the storm abated and they reached home safely.

In the middle ages seamen had various saints to whom they called for help. The Scottish merchant colony in Bruges erected an altar to St Ninian, and paid tolls on freight money to support a chaplain who said masses for their safe journeys and the good of their souls.

Sometimes the holy man did more than just bless or pray. In 1892 the fishing fleet was out at Lindisfarne when the sea rose unexpectedly. The Reverent Bryson whistled up a scratch crew that included his own sexton, a handful of sick seamen and a fish merchant and called on the women to help launch the lifeboat. The seas off Northumberland can be as dangerous as any in the world, but the reverent managed to shepherd his flock of boats back to the safety of Lindisfarne harbour.

All these are only anecdotes from a vast store of stories, but they show something of the relationship between religion and the sea. Even sea shanties can have a religious tinge, with the famous *Fine Girl You Are* relating to the Holy ground in Liverpool. This area, the Scotland Road red-light district, was owned by the Roman Catholic Church. And that should be as strange as anything at sea.

Chapter Sixteen
Limeys and Scurvy

While most English language sea histories concentrate on the experiences of sailors from Britain or the United States, other nations have a maritime history every bit as interesting. In European terms, England and Lowland Scotland were relative late comers to the field of navigation; Gaelic and Norse seafarers had ventured north and west to the Faroes, Iceland and perhaps Greenland; Scandinavians had probed the great rivers of the East, and Italians had sailed just about everywhere before British ships probed into new waters. In the 15th and 16th centuries, the Iberian nations of Spain and Portugal were the masters of the sea as they broke all previous boundaries to discover new routes to the east, south and west.

Most of these voyages were for profit. Spanish and Portuguese galleons sailed the golden seas to enrich their mother country and those of the crew that survived. Their treasure galleons became legend as they furrowed the vast new oceans with cargoes of silks and spices, gold and silver, damask and jewels and legend. True, there were occasional losses to buccaneers, pirates or royal enemies, but mostly the galleons had other concerns. As with every seaman throughout history, the masters worried about the weather, and they also lived in mortal dread of disease.

Of all the Spanish vessels, the mighty Manila Galleon, the 'China ship' or *naos de China* that crossed the Pacific Ocean in an annual pilgrimage to the God of Greed, was the most important. This ship loaded all the riches that Spain had scoured from the East and gathered in the Philippines and carried them to Acapulco in Mexico in a voyage that lasted six months. The ship, or sometimes ships, was packed to excess, with bales and bundles stowed in the holds and on deck, in companionways and cabins and even in the ship's boats. In modern terms it would be difficult to calculate the value of even one of these cargoes, but millions would be an underestimate and tens of millions probably not too much. In 1587 the English captain Thomas Cavendish captured the Manila Galleon *Santa Ana*, hanged a priest, landed most of the 300 crew and passengers on the hostile shore of South America and looted her. Crossing the Pacific, Indian Ocean and sailing up the Atlantic took a year, but when Cavendish sailed up the Thames in 1588 his *Desire* had sails of blue damask and every member of the crew wore a gold chain.

As well as treasure, the China Ship carried colonists returning home and officials whose terms of office had ended. Despite months of preparations by some of the most experienced and skilled mariners in the world, all the passengers feared the voyage. They knew that they would face storms. There were typhoons off Taiwan, bitter cold in the North Pacific and incessant gales off the North American Coast. Gemelli Careri, an Italian termed it 'the longest and most dreadful' voyage 'of any in the world for the terrible Tempests that happen and for the desperate Diseases.'

In 250 years, storms sunk 30 galleons; their rotted timbers lie on the sea bed or on the jagged coral of sea battered islands. At the turn of the 16th and 17th century, storms kept *Santa Margarita* in the Western Pacific for eight months before finally showing mercy and throwing her onto the Ladrones with less than one fifth of her crew still breathing. Disease was as bad. Scurvy and ship fevers robbed the crew of their will and ability to work.

It was disease that created one of the true ghost ships of the ocean, for on one occasion it killed the entire crew of the Manila galleon. Shocked Spanish sailors discovered the ship surging on, sails fully set, with a crew of corpses to tend the treasure of the king.

Scurvy, of course, was international. It killed without malice and without mercy, so men of every seafaring nation died horribly if they remained more than a few scant weeks away from land. Scurvy softened the gums so that a man's teeth would loosen and fall. It created black sores beneath the skin, weakened the heart and re-opened old wounds. Stricken men could not concentrate on their work, but dropped helpless to the deck, unless a kindly shipmate carried them to their hammock, where they lay until they died, or until somebody accidentally fed them fresh food.

If war killed its thousands, scurvy killed its tens of thousands. During the Seven Year War of 1757 to 1763, an estimated 1,512 British seamen died in action, but over 133,000 died of disease. The world will never know how many shipwrecks were caused when disease enfeebled the crew so they could no longer work the ship. Surgeons and ship-masters were baffled how to cure this mysterious disease; prayers failed to help, and although there were certain wells, such as the healing well of St Mary's in Montrose, which offered a cure, they seldom worked either. For centuries scurvy con-trolled the seas far more effectively than any man of war.

In the 300 years following 1500, more seamen died of disease than through all other causes com-bined, yet the terrifying tragedy was not in the number of deaths, but in the fact that they were preventable. As early as the mid-14th century the Arab traveller Ibn Battutta noted that Chinese seamen carried 'greenstuffs, vegetables and ginger' with them on long voyages, but nobody realised the significance. In 1636 John Woodall's book *The Surgeon's Mate* recommended orange juice to cure scurvy, but 158 years and around 850,000 fatalities later, ships still sailed with the scourge of scurvy crouched in the scuppers.

To cure scurvy, ascorbic acid, or vitamin C, is required. It takes only a daily ounce of citrus juice to control or cure the terrible disease that killed so many seamen for so long. Among the most celebrated disasters due to scurvy was Anson's cruise of 1740, when he was sent with six ships to intercept the Manila Galleon. Scurvy more than decimated his men, so his squadron was reduced to a single vessel, but still he captured a galleon whose treasure filled thirty two wagons when it eventually reached London and made Anson rich for life. During the voyage, Anson lost six men from hostile fire, but over 1300 from disease.

In 1747, James Lind, a Scottish naval surgeon, supervised a controlled experiment with twelve scurvy-ridden seamen in Salisbury. While he treated ten with the more common remedies, such as elixir vitriol, vinegar and seawater, he allowed the remaining pair with two oranges and a lemon each day. Within week, the final pair was fit for duty. Lind published his findings in 1753, yet after a ten-week cruise in 1779, the Channel Fleet landed over 2400 scorbutic seamen. Not all ship's masters, however, were so short sighted. When Captain Cook voyaged to the same Pacific Ocean that had ravaged both Spanish and British fleets, he insisted that his ship was kept clean and issued anti-scorbutic foods such as pickled cabbage and orange juice. Cook used the threat of the cat to encourage men to eat a healthy diet, so that there was no scurvy on his *Endeavour*.

By the beginning of the 19th century, British ships were obliged by law to carry lime juice. The original requirement was for lemon juice, but the names of both fruit were often interchangeable. Limes were not so suitable, so that scurvy often appeared on long voyages, including those of the Arctic whalers. However, seamen were often to blame for their own misfortunes, for it was not unknown for scorbutic men to rub lime juice onto the sores rather than apply it internally.

The world had changed a lot since the galleons of Spain struggled across the Pacific, but despite the wars and political conniving, it was the work of a dedicated surgeon that had made the seas safer for sailors. Not until 1912 did scientists discover vitamins, and really understand the nature of scurvy, and by that time British seamen were known throughout the world as 'limeys.' The name has remained, while the scourge of scurvy, like the legendary galleons of Spain, has receded to a memory.

Chapter Seventeen
What If?

Jean-Francois Galoup, Comte de La Perouse was one of the finest seamen that 18th century France produced. He served the sea from a very young age, and when just eighteen took part in the Battle of Quiberon Bay in 1759. He was on board *Formidable* when the British captured her amidst remarkable scenes of slaughter, and commanded vessels during the War of American Independence.

Small wonder then, that La Perouse should be given command of a voyage of exploration. There were a number of volunteers, from which only those best qualified were selected, and in 1785 La Perouse left Brest in *Boussole*, with *Astrolabe* as consort, to search for the Pacific end of the North West Passage between the Atlantic and Asia. He sailed at a time when French prestige was at its' height. France had been a crucial player in securing American independence, the British had been humbled and all was right with the world. Now all that remained was for a French navigator to exceed the exploits of Cook by finding the North West Passage, a prize that had eluded generations of British seamen.

La Perouse spent six weeks off the coast of Alaska before shocking weather drove him, under storm staysails and little else, for Hawaii, where he was the first known European to sight Necker Island. After that, with the Passage closed for a season, La Perouse followed his secondary orders to investigate the north east coasts of Asia. He had a fifth of the world to explore and two fine ships; what could be better for a gallant French captain? He nosed along the coast of Korea from Quelpart Island nearly to where Vladivostok now sits, discovered the Strait between Sakhalin and Japan and cast anchor in Petropavlovsk in Kamchatka.

So far the expedition had been moderately successful, with new islands and a new strait discovered, and some hundreds of miles of coastline explored. La Perouse sailed south for the sun, dropping anchor in Mauna in the Samoan Islands. These islands have a unique beauty, but in the late 18th century they were home to some of the most savage people in the world. With swords edged with shark teeth and clubs carved from hard wood, the islanders fell on a French landing party, killing the captain of *Astrolabe* and ten of his matelots.

Leaving these sinister shores, La Perouse steered for the Friendly Islands, touched at Norfolk Island and then, on the 26 January 1788, beat into Botany Bay against a fresh breeze. After so long away from Europe, La Perouse was astonished to see a squadron of European ships, flying the multi-crossed flag of the British Union. No doubt there were initial worries; after all La Perouse had spent much of his adult life fighting the British, but any war was far from here. 'All Europeans are countrymen,' he noted in his log, 'at such a distance from home.'

The British were not quite so sure. Captain Arthur Philip commanded this, the First Fleet that carried convicts to found and settle Australia. The

British smiled politely and offered La Perouse a handshake and nothing else; they claimed they could not spare stores, food, sails or cordage. As The French watched in some amusement, the First Fleet left the harbour with a fine display of ineptitude, with vessels colliding and others barely avoiding scraping their bottoms off the rocks. Surely La Perouse must have hidden his smile, for after helping France remove one set of colonies from Britannia, he was now witnessing the beginnings of another fiasco. He did not smile later, when escaped convicts begged to be taken aboard his ship. He sent them back to the labour gang and flogging triangle while he prepared for the next stage of his voyage.

Sometime after the 7th February 1788, La Perouse lifted anchor and sailed into the Pacific. No European saw him, his ships or his crews alive again. Not until 1826 did Captain Dillon discover the wreckage of his vessels on the reefs at Vanokoro Island in the Santa Cruz group.

This tale of exploration has many facets. It shows the enterprise of France at a time just before the Revolution altered her forever. It shows the skill and bravery of European mariners operating thousands of miles from home, on expeditions that lasted for years. It shows the rivalry and similarity of European mariners in distant waters. However, there is one other point. Among the hopeful volunteers who applied to join the expedition was one Napoleon Bonaparte, a young artillery officer from Corsica. If he had been accepted, the whole course of the world may have changed. What would have happened of Bonaparte had not been present to guide the course of the French Revolution? If there had been no genius to guide the French armies? No French victories, no wearing down of Continental Europe, no Waterloo and rise of Britain as the dominant power?

Or perhaps history would have been created in an unimaginable way? What if Bonaparte had taken control of the French ships, taken over Australia and challenged Britain from twelve thousand miles away?

The possibilities are endless; they are surely among the strangest tales of the sea.

Made in the USA
Middletown, DE
09 March 2021